SHREWSBURY

Archaeological discoveries from a medieval town

Nigel Baker

Shropshire
Books

Cover illustration: Detail from a panoramic oil painting of Shrewsbury from the east, painted some time in the later 1630s or early 1640s. The picture shows the town wall and a tower in the Dogpole area. Behind are St Julian's church (left) and St Alkmund's (right).

© Text Nigel Baker 2003
ISBN: 0-903802-82-1

Cover and book design: The Graphic Terrace
Managing Editor: Helen Sample
Published by Shropshire Books, the publishing division of
Shropshire County Council's Community & Environment Services Department

Printed in Great Britain by Livesey Limited

About the author

Nigel Baker is a freelance archaeologist who has worked in Shrewsbury on and off since 1978, latterly on the Shrewsbury Urban Archaeological Strategy programme. He has a similar long-standing relationship with the city of Worcester and is currently engaged on the Strategy programme there. In addition to local-authority and strategic planning archaeology, the author also undertakes consultancy and fieldwork for owners and developers, builders, architects, engineers and other planning professionals in the Shrewsbury area and the west midlands.

Acknowledgements and picture credits

This book is in large part a distillation of the research of many archaeologists, historians and architectural historians who have worked on Shrewsbury in recent years. A particular debt is owed to the historian Bill Champion, for much of the historical information regarding the medieval and Tudor town and its buildings. A further debt is owed to many of the author's friends and colleagues, including Dorothy Cromarty, Hugh Hannaford, Ernie Jenks, James Lawson, Madge Moran and David Pannett, for many illuminating conversations and for generously sharing the results of their own discoveries. The author is also grateful to the staff of the Shropshire Records & Research Centre, the Shrewsbury Museums Service, and the Shropshire County Archaeological Service and Historic Environment Record. Amongst the other organisations whose work is represented in the following pages particular mention must be made of Birmingham Archaeology (Birmingham University Field Archaeology Unit), Marches Archaeology Ltd and Richard K Morriss & Associates.

A significant proportion of the discoveries reported here was made in the course of the Shrewsbury Urban Archaeological Strategy programme, funded by English Heritage and undertaken on behalf of Shrewsbury & Atcham Borough Council.

Finally, the hidden history of the town would have remained hidden were it not for the generous co-operation of the residents and business community of Shrewsbury who allowed access to their properties, buildings and cellars.

Thanks are also due to the following for their kind permission to reproduce illustrations:

Shropshire Archives: pp. 7, 9, 18, 20, 23, 25, 26, 28, 30, 31, 32, 33, 36-7, 38, 39, 42, 51, 53,
Shrewsbury Museum & Art Gallery: pp. 3, 4, 63
The late Phillip Barker and Peter Barker: p. 21
Birmingham Archaeology: p. 49
Peter Napier and Richard K Morriss: p. 56
From a private collection/photo by Alan Snell: p.8 and cover

CONTENTS

An aeriel view of Pride Hill. Even the huge shopping centres of the 1980s (Darwin Centre left, Pride Hill Centre right) are fitted into a framework of ancient property boundaries, elements of which are probably pre-Norman

Introduction

Shrewsbury is an archaeological site just as much as any ancient ruined city. The difference, of course, is that Shrewsbury is a thriving town and has existed as an urban community without interruption for at least a thousand years. Continuity with the past is present in many forms. Almost every town-centre street can be traced back in the records at least seven hundred years and there are signs that many are much older. Shops built in the 1450s still function more or less as their builders intended. The local authority, the Borough Council, is the lineal descendant of the bailiffs and council of twelve Theynesmen of the 12th century. Modern shopping centres have to be designed to fit sites whose property boundaries were first staked-out before the Norman Conquest for the greater convenience of grazing cattle (see opposite). It is possible to sit in a town-centre pub, relaxing on an oak settle by the fire, conscious of an unbroken succession of customers stretching back three or more centuries, each past generation alive in the memories of the next. But Shrewsbury is not just a tourist town, deserted out of season and out of hours, it is a busy, modern, county town with a diverse economic base. Perhaps because the past is everywhere it is scarcely regarded as exceptional - but it is.

Over the last thirty or so years there have been many discoveries and many new insights into Shrewsbury's remote past. 'Rescue archaeology', excavation in advance of redevelopment, has brought in much new information. Historians have been exploring hitherto untapped archival resources offering, for the first time, property-by-property histories of much of the town centre. And research into the town's historic buildings has been taking place: archaeologists and architectural historians have analysed individual buildings in the course of repair work, and a programme of dendrochronological (tree-ring) dating has produced precise dates - and thus potential links to documented owners or builders - for many of the town's timber-framed buildings. Because of its importance as an historic town, Shrewsbury was selected in the early 1990s to be part of a national archaeological strategy sponsored by English Heritage. This aimed to produce, for each of the thirty or so towns covered, a new computer database of all archaeological discoveries, a published assessment volume for each town, and new local government policies for the historic environment, each stage tailored to the requirements and special character of each place.

The turn of the century has seen further excavation, some in previously unexplored parts of the town, and the first ever investigations at the castle. The aim of this book is to present, in summary form, for the first time, a few important aspects of this new knowledge of Shrewsbury's past.

The construction site for the Charles Darwin shopping centre in 1987. Medieval sandstone cellars have been exposed by the demolition of the building above (the former Woolworth's of 1927). Seventy Steps runs up the left hand side of the site, cutting across the cellar on the Pride Hill frontage

A brief archaeological history

Neither two centuries of historical scholarship nor a generation of professional archaeological excavation have been able to solve, with any certainty, the mystery of the origins of Shrewsbury. There are a few hard facts and a few more plausible historical theories, but ultimately, the Dark Age origins of Shrewsbury remain dark.

Shrewsbury, looking east across the Severn loop. The Welsh Bridge is in the foreground, English Bridge in the background. The great curving arc of the medieval town walls is still visible between them

One certainty is that Shrewsbury was not the first regional capital in the area. The invading Roman army, taking control of the tribal territory of the *Cornovii* in the mid-50s AD, built a legionary fortress overlooking the Severn about seven miles downstream of the site where Shrewsbury would later develop. The fortress attracted civilian settlement which, by degrees, grew to become the tribal capital, *Viroconium Cornoviorum*, the fourth largest city of Roman Britain. Wroxeter, to give it its later English name, did not go into terminal decline immediately upon the withdrawal of the Roman legions in the early 400s: excavations in the old city centre have shown that some sort of town life continued there for generations. The public baths buildings were maintained for an apparently numerous public for years before being turned into an open-air market. And then in the 6th century, perhaps in the mid-500s, the central area was re-planned with timber-framed buildings dominated by a large, two-storey, villa-like building that may have been the base of whoever, or whatever authority, then ran the city. This final episode in the long life of Wroxeter was probably winding down in the mid- to late 7th century. Outside, farming no doubt continued in the rich agricultural hinterland, possibly sheltered from raids from the Welsh highlands by a linear frontier earthwork - Wat's Dyke - now thought to have been built as early as c.500AD.

The ruins of Roman Wroxeter. There was no mass transfer of population from Wroxeter to Shrewsbury. As the importance of the former gradually diminished in the years before 700AD, there are signs of activity on the site that would in time become Shrewsbury

Around the early 7th century the English, or Anglo-Saxon, influence was becoming stronger in the region which, by means unknown to us, passed out of British (or Welsh) control and became part of the English kingdom of Mercia. The episode was dramatised two centuries later in Welsh poetry featuring Cynddylan, a prince of the kingdom of Powys, and his sister Heledd. In one famous scene Cynddylan laments the destruction of his hall at a place called Pengwern (*Llys Bengwern*).
In the 12th century this was identified by the chronicler Gerald of Wales as Shrewsbury.
Modern scholarship now suggests that the events in the poems are more likely to have taken place at a later date in the Lichfield area and to have been transposed in time and space to a more dramatic setting: one which was understood to have once been Welsh, but which by then was English. If Gerald of Wales had any real evidence at all to equate Pengwern with Shrewsbury, it is lost to us, though the legend persists.

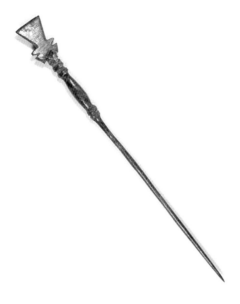

It is however very likely that something was happening on the site of Shrewsbury by c.700AD. The origin of both St Mary's Church and Old St Chad's appear to lie in this period. Both were original monastic - minster churches, served by a community of priests charged with responsibility for preaching over a wide area of the surrounding countryside. In fact the territory controlled by each was so large that it is almost inconceivable that they were founded at any much later date, when the countryside was more populous and ownership of it more fragmented. St Mary's was traditionally held to have been founded by the kings of Mercia, St Chad's by an early bishop of Lichfield. Monastic foundations of this 'heroic' period of the early English Church usually sought isolated or marginal locations, and in this respect the Shrewsbury site was ideal. Each church occupied a prominent hilltop within what was virtually an island, cut off by the river-loop from the outside world. This place lay towards the western edge of the Mercian kingdom, on the boundary between the medieval dioceses of Lichfield and Hereford - which each reflected an earlier tribal grouping. There may even have been an element of colonisation behind such foundations in this frontier district. Just possibly it was the final, deliberate, nail in the coffin of any last vestiges of power still clinging to Roman *Viroconium*.

This fine group of historic buildings off St Alkmund's Place, part of the former King's Market, may conceal the site of an Anglo-Saxon royal palace

How, and how fast, this 'monastic island', if that is what it was, turned into a town is one of the greatest outstanding problems of Shrewsbury's archaeology. For hard evidence we must fast-forward two centuries, to the year 901. In that year a royal charter was issued, granting land to Wenlock Priory by Aethelred and Aethelflaed (his wife) of Mercia, witnessed by thirteen Mercian notables. The charter was issued in *civitate Scrobbensis*: this may be translated as the city of the district called the Scrub. Slightly later Shrewsbury was referred to as *Scrobbesbyrig* - the fort or *burh* (borough) of the Scrub. For it to have been called a 'city' is significant - it denotes a place of political and religious importance; for the charter to have been signed there at all shows that there must have been a royal hall somewhere on the site by 901.

A handful of further incidental references is all that the documentary record can contribute to pre-Conquest Shrewsbury. It was the county town by soon after 1000 AD. Coins had been minted there since the reign of Aethelstan (925-939), a fact that confirms that early Shrewsbury was fortified (by law, mints had to be in fortified places). But it is the account of the town given by Domesday Book that reveals most. By the time of the Norman Conquest there were four churches within the river-loop - St Mary's, St Chad's, St Alkmund's and St Juliana's - all of them wealthy and important. There were also 252 tax-paying households, a figure translated by historians into a likely total population of around 1,200 people. Domesday also records some of the changes brought about by the Conquest, including the destruction of fifty-one houses by the building of the castle (see p.13).

Archaeology can add further details of the Saxon town, but nothing approaching a comprehensive picture. Archaeological remains of the period are generally identified from their association with a distinctive type of pottery known as Stafford-type ware, after the only production site so far discovered. The problem with this pottery is that it was produced over a period of about two hundred and fifty years, from soon after c.800AD until about the time of the Conquest, and there is as yet no reliable way of distinguishing early 9th-century sherds from mid-11th century. As a result, measuring the growth of Saxon Shrewsbury is, and probably always will be, extremely difficult.

Anglo-Saxon pottery, probably manufactured in Stafford between c.800 and c.1000AD. Found in excavations below the Castle Gates Library

Nevertheless, Stafford Ware has now been found over most of the river loop, from Castle Foregate to Barker Street and to the bottom of Wyle Cop, and in the eastern suburb under the Abbey. Saxon Shrewsbury, by the time of the Norman Conquest, cannot have been much smaller than the medieval and later town centre. Filled-in back-yard latrine pits are the most common find of this period, and have been excavated on the McDonald's site on Pride Hill, under the Castle Gates Library buildings, the Prince Rupert Hotel, and elsewhere. A superb rubbish dump containing food debris, metal-working residues, and pottery from as far away as East Anglia has also been excavated from an old floodplain channel at the bottom of Wyle Cop (the Century Cinema site). Structural remains are limited to a fragment of a timber house excavated in 1990 near the corner of Pride Hill and the High Street (see p.47), and the revelation, in the 1860s, of the foundations of a Saxon church beneath the floor of St Mary's (p.28). The town defences - a vital protection against raiding by the Danes or the Welsh - have yet to be discovered, but probably lie across the neck of the river-loop under Meadow Place and the castle (see p.14).

Remains of the medieval town wall on Meadow Place. The Anglo-Saxon defences probably followed the same line, blocking the landward approach to the town from the north

In all probability the remains of the Saxon town are everywhere around us, but cannot usually be distinguished for what they are because they remain in use in the present townscape. Most of the town-centre streets were probably already ancient when they (and their often-inexplicable names, like Mardol) first appear in the documentary record after c.1200. Landscape analysis has suggested that many of the modern property boundaries of premises on streets like Pride Hill, Mardol and Dogpole originated in this period and have remained in use and respected by neighbours ever since. At the bottom of Mardol, around the King's Head, is a series of properties with a very distinctive curve, originally designed to give the occupants access to the river Severn at the rear. The area has not been excavated but was probably a tiny industrial district for trades that required such access - like tanners, dyers, watermen and boat-builders. Bigger, longer plots ran back from the frontage of Pride Hill, down the slope and into Raven Meadows, some reaching to the river, giving a trading frontage at one end and space for grazing and watering livestock at the other; similar plots were also to be found along Dogpole.

Following the Norman Conquest, Shrewsbury was secured for the invaders by the construction of the castle at the entrance to the river-loop. The county town became the centre of a new earldom, almost a semi-autonomous state, charged (along with Cheshire and Herefordshire) with the aggressive pacification of the Welsh border. The Normanisation of English Shrewsbury proceeded relentlessly. Earl Roger of Montgomery adopted the suburban property and private church of a wealthy Englishman on the east bank of the Severn and began building an abbey there for a community of Norman monks. Frenchmen were settled in the town.

By 1121 the Severn was bridged in two places, probably on or close to the sites of the Welsh and English Bridges. A generation later the ancient Saxon minster churches were completely rebuilt, and work was probably in progress at the castle, rebuilding the earthwork and timber defences with the masonry walls that still survive. But, apart from the major public buildings and churches, virtually nothing is known of the changing physical character of the town in this century. It must however have been growing: by c.1200 not only were most of the town-centre streets in existence, so too were the suburbs, Castle Foregate, Frankwell, Coton Hill, Coleham and Abbey Foregate all appearing in the historical record by this time.

The 13th-century town is much more clearly defined, historically and archaeologically. Catastrophe struck in 1215, in the form of Welsh forces under Llewellyn the Great, who captured the town and its castle without difficulty, approaching from the rear, via Abbey Foregate. Instructions soon followed from the Crown to the citizens of Shrewsbury to defend themselves properly, and by 1220 work had begun on the town walls. Although largely completed by 1242, repairs, additions and modifications to the walls were to go on for many years to come - not only from military necessity, but because the walls and gates became, as elsewhere, a symbol of the town's independence and self-government, proudly displayed on the borough seal. Within the walls, the population grew, in numbers (probably around 5000 by c.1300) and in wealth. The town's leading citizens were numbered amongst the country's business elite, with offices in London and connections, as wool exporters and financiers, on the continent and at court, and they began to build their Shrewsbury town houses in stone. By 1334 Shrewsbury was ranked the seventh wealthiest provincial town in England.

The Black Death hit Shrewsbury in 1349 and, although statistics were not collected, probably wiped out rather more than a third of the population. The long-term effect on the town is uncertain; although there are signs of commercial resilience, with traffic still pouring through the town gates on market days. The economy was changing, too: Shrewsbury was becoming a cloth manufacturing town rather than a centre for wool exports, but was beginning to face competition from other, much smaller, centres like Welshpool and Oswestry for the growing trade in Welsh cloth. The town faced new problems at the beginning of the 15th century. A fire had devastated Wyle Cop in 1393 and rebuilding was still taking place in the 1420s. In c.1404 Owain Glyndwr's forces raided and burnt the suburbs; in 1407 the town petitioned the king for a remission of its taxes. The Battle of Shrewsbury of 1403 was an event of the greatest national significance, but appears to have left no visible impact on the town. The surviving physical evidence, particularly from the first three-quarters of the century, is of an apparently buoyant urban economy. Most of the town's surviving fifty or so medieval houses date from this period, including some its most famous buildings, like the Abbot's House on Butcher Row (built 1457-9) and the Henry Tudor House on Wyle Cop (built 1423-30);

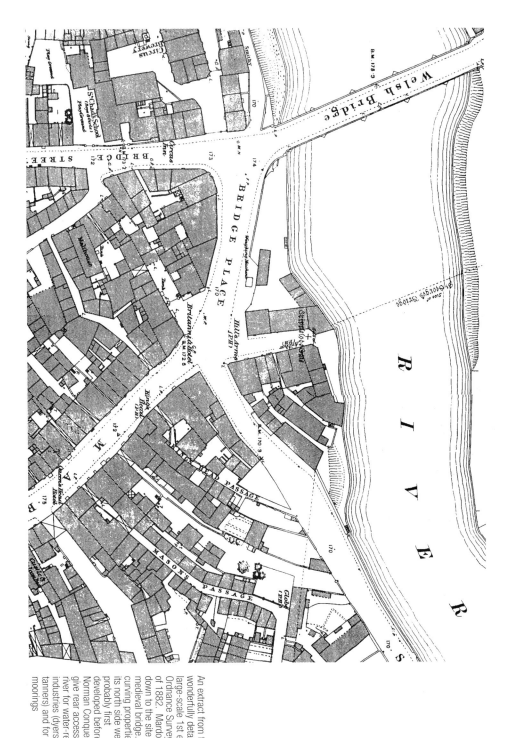

An extract from the wonderfully detailed large-scale 1st edition Ordnance Survey plans of 1882. Mardol runs down to the site of the medieval bridge. The curving properties on its north side were probably first developed before the Norman Conquest to give rear access to the river for water-related industries (dyers, tanners) and for moorings

The medieval town wall and a tower, behind Dogpole. A detail from an early panorama of Shrewsbury from the east, painted in the 1630s or early 1640s

many buildings included speculatively built shop units. The local economy began, however, to slip into serious recession in the 1460s and it, and population levels, remained stagnant for almost a century. Construction activity declined, and the late medieval townscape must have become increasingly shabby and run-down. The Reformation also had a dramatic impact, the town losing the three friaries around its walls in the 1530s and Shrewsbury Abbey in 1540. The old fortifications too were in decline: the castle was becoming ruinous and some sections of the town wall had been built over by houses.

As always, it is periods of prosperity, change and rebuilding that leave the strongest imprint on the physical or archaeological record. And so, in Shrewsbury, it is the decades between 1560 and 1630 that are etched indelibly into the streetscape. The great majority of the town's 'black and white' timber-framed buildings date to these years, which were marked by an economic boom and a rapidly expanding urban and suburban population. Late 16th-century Shrewsbury was dominated by the Drapers' Company, whose richer members bought cloth from the farmer-weavers at the Oswestry and Welshpool markets, had it sheared and finished in Shrewsbury and arranged its delivery to London for sale. Many or most of the fine houses of this period were built by merchants belonging to this guild. The same individuals were also active in town government, and were responsible for the construction of some of the great public buildings of the time, such as the Old Market Hall of 1596 and the Grammar School buildings of 1595 and 1627, now part of the Castle Gates Library.

The Grammar School buildings on Castle Gates in the 19th century, before the school (Shrewsbury School) moved out to Kingsland

After the mid-17th century the direction of Shrewsbury's economy again began to shift, slowly but irrevocably away from manufacturing and towards consumption and what would now be called the service sector. County gentry families began to look on the town as an appropriate place in which to socialise and spend time and money. A few town houses had been built in brick in the early part of the century (like Rowley's Mansion) but, by the end, brick construction was more or less mandatory for polite houses. So too were gardens. The Earl of Bradford's town house of the 1690s (later the Guildhall) on Dogpole had 'hanging gardens' terraced down the slope behind. Walks and gardens were laid out for public recreation at the Abbey, over the former monks' cemetery, and at the Quarry. The scene was gradually being set for another golden age - the late 18th century, the Shrewsbury of personalities like Thomas Farnolls Pritchard, the architect, Thomas Telford, surveyor and engineer, John Ashby, lawyer, political agent and builder of the Lion Hotel, Charles Bage, builder-owner of the world's first iron-framed mill and Dr Erasmus Darwin, grandfather of the man whose influence would spread far, far beyond the town of his birth.

The shape
of Shrewsbury

There is much more to the site and shape of Shrewsbury than the Severn river loop. The ancient town centre straddles two hills separated by a shallow valley followed by the High Street. The southern hill is more of a ridge, extending west to east from the present St Chad's Church to Old St Chad's and Belmont. The northern hill rises steeply from the High Street up towards St Alkmund's and St Julian's and thence gently to the highest point close to St Mary's. From there, the ground level descends gradually to the north, into the mouth of the river loop, where stands the castle. The ground drops away sharply west and north of the castle towards the station and Castle Foregate, but the effect is exaggerated by the castle earthworks.

The northern high ground drops away sharply towards the river to the north-west and east, at the back of Pride Hill and Dogpole respectively; these escarpments add to the natural defensibility of the river-bound site and were formerly surmounted by the medieval town wall. Below, lie the river and its floodplain. The latter is widest on the north-west, the area known as Raven Meadows, where a prehistoric river meander cut deep into the escarpment. The higher, well-drained ground extends down to the water's edge at two points, both at places where the river was broad, shallow and easily bridged. This, however, is the natural landscape.

But Shrewsbury has existed on this spot for a millennium and has had to adapt its site as it has grown: archaeology is beginning to be able to document the consequences. First, the natural gradients have been adapted for dense, urban living by terracing - cutting in and building out level platforms for houses, their backyards and gardens. Were it possible to see the town with its buildings removed, some areas would . look not unlike mediterranean vineyards, with terraces and their retaining walls conforming to the natural slopes.

A view from St John's Hill looking north up Pride Hill. Across the shallow valley bottom between them (Shoplatch) a stream once ran west towards Barker Street

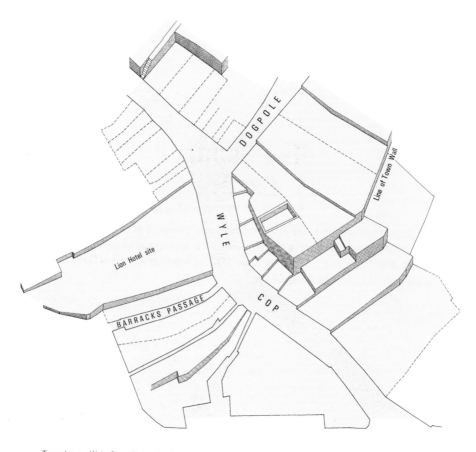

Terracing on Wyle Cop. These level platforms on which all the present buildings stand were built on the natural slope sometime before the 15th century

The process of engineering the gradients - controlling erosion as well as making more room - was well underway by c.1300.

Second, low-lying wet areas were subject to reclamation, at least at strategic points where there was pressure on space. A large natural pool and peat-bog in the central valley, in the area of the Square, was deliberately reclaimed, probably in the first half of the 13th century, in what may have been the town's first great local government civil engineering project (see p.43). Floodplain and low-lying areas around the bridges were also reclaimed and levels raised against the threat of flooding, particularly after a climatic deterioration that began roughly c.1300. Such processes could produce localised changes of some magnitude: levels were raised in the area of the Square by some three metres (ten feet), and at the bottom of Wyle Cop by a similar amount. Much greater changes occurred in the 19th and 20th centuries, particularly in the 1960s-1980s, with commercial buildings of unprecedented bulk disguising some parts of the natural terrain.

Shrewsbury Castle

Shrewsbury Castle is one of the best-preserved monuments in western England to the turbulent, bloody decade that followed the Norman Conquest, and to the suppression of English townspeople and their Welsh neighbours nine hundred years ago. And, as with so much else in Shrewsbury's past, there is much more to it than first meets the eye.

Shrewsbury Castle; the surviving Inner Bailey with the hall on the left and the Norman motte disguised by trees on the right

The castle was built by William the Conqueror within three or four years of his victory at Hastings and is first heard of in 1069. William and his Norman army were campaigning in northern England when a revolt broke out in the western midlands. The royal fortress at Shrewsbury was besieged by a local force led by Edric the Wild, one of the wealthiest landowners in the county before the Conquest. The rebels - Welshmen, and men from Chester and Shrewsbury, 'and other untameable Englishmen' - burnt the town and retired before William could send reinforcements. The incident, recorded by Orderic Vitalis, the monastic historian baptised at Atcham in 1075 and educated in Shrewsbury, shows the castle in its original role. It was not built to protect the town: its primary purpose was to dominate it - to suppress rebellion and monitor and intimidate the urban population.

The castle of this time was an earthwork castle, defended by timber structures that were replaced in stone and do not survive, and by massive earthworks - ramparts and ditches - that do survive, buried or disguised by later phases of the castle or by the growth of the town over them. The core of the early Norman castle was the motte, the great earth mound, twenty metres higher than the bailey, much higher above the river. On this stood a great timber tower that would have provided a final strongpoint in case of a determined assault and, more routinely, would have been high enough to enable the garrison to maintain surveillance over the entire town. Potential trouble, like hostile gatherings in the market places or movements across the fords, could be spotted instantly from this 11th-century equivalent of a military satellite, towering perhaps a hundred feet above the single-storey town buildings. The motte survives, though one side of it had eroded and slipped into the river by 1255 and its great wooden tower collapsed c.1270. Since about 1790 the motte has been crowned by Laura's Tower, a summerhouse-folly built by Thomas Telford for the castle's owner and named after his daughter. Ground-penetrating radar on the top of the motte has shown that it contains the buried foundations of stone buildings; radar also showed that the parapet walls around the top are built on medieval walls two metres thick. The foundations of a late 13th-century turret can be seen protruding from the present parapet wall at the base of Laura's Tower.

At the foot of the motte was the inner bailey, and this too is extremely well preserved. The stone curtain walls that now enclose it were probably built in the mid-12th century, though they have been repeatedly rebuilt and repaired since. Their crenellated parapets were originally medieval, but were probably rebuilt by Thomas Telford, and then again rebuilt in 1887. The walls distract attention from the original early Norman ramparts on which they stand. These are best seen from inside the inner bailey - grassed or planted earth banks rising two to four metres above the level of the interior, though levels inside the inner bailey have risen, disguising much of their height. It may well be that much of the hill on which the castle appears to stand is actually artificial, though the effect is exaggerated by the lowering of levels at the railway station below for the addition of its bottom storey in 1902-3. The rampart on the town side of the inner bailey has been lost, presumably removed when the present entrance gate was built in the mid-12th century (the second gateway, beside it, was inserted in the 1860s having been salvaged from the nearby chapel of St Nicholas). Outside, where the artillery pieces now stand, the sloping courses of the sandstone wall that once connected the castle to the upper town gate (across Castle Gates by the library buildings) show how much the ground profile has changed; there was almost certainly once a substantial ditch separating the inner bailey from the town.

In front of the castle was a zone that had been cleared of housing and was to become the castle's outer bailey; Domesday Book records that fifty-one houses had been destroyed in the process of building the castle. In 1978 excavations under Rigg's Hall (the timber-framed building which now houses the children's section of the Castle Gates Library) found remains of these in the form of a latrine pit, quarry pits, and large quantities of late Saxon pottery. The whole area was isolated from the town by another outer defence, probably in the form of a ditch and rampart dug across Castle Street at the narrowest part of the high ground, just north of Windsor Place. This has long since disappeared but can be reconstructed from topographical clues, documentary evidence, and Victorian records of discoveries made when digging for cellars. Most recently, archaeologists

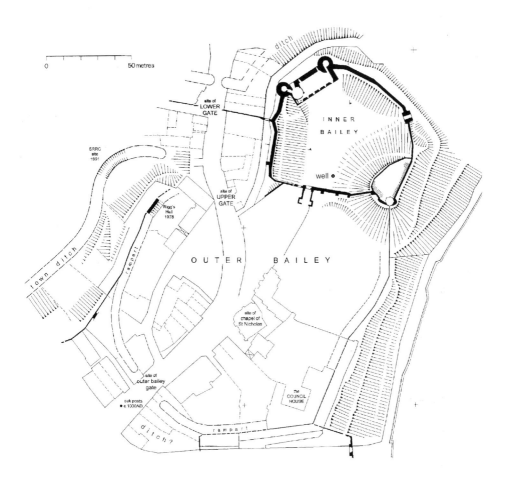

An archaeological plan of the castle showing the extent of the former Outer Bailey and the outer defences crossing Castle Street

monitoring the renewal of a water main along the street found a row of preserved oak posts carbon-dated to c.1030 - perhaps part of a bridge crossing the outer ditch, perhaps part of the housing cleared for the castle. The outer bailey was still distinct from the town in the early 13th century but had disappeared by the end.

The present stone buildings of the castle belong to later centuries. The hall, sometimes known as the Keep, together with its great flanking circular towers, was probably built in the middle of the 13th century. Accounts of the period record the building of the King's chamber and tower(s); the hall may be the building referred to, but later alterations have removed much evidence of the original design. The principal space was then, as now, at first-floor level, open to the roof, with an undercroft beneath, probably for secure storage. Whether the hall was originally an undivided space, or whether a former partition provided a private chamber at the west end, is uncertain. The towers at each end offered further, more private, accommodation. In the base of each was an unlit room; that in the east tower was probably a dungeon. Each tower has further rooms at first- and second-floor

The castle hall, cut into the Norman earth ramparts, probably in the mid-13th century

level. The second-floor room in the west tower was obviously something special, as it was provided with a lobby with a stone vaulted roof. Similarities with better-known castle buildings of the period, Conway in particular, suggest that this room may have been a private chapel provided for the king at this more private 'high' end of the building. But, although there is a replica medieval fireplace in the north wall of the hall that may be on the site of an original, in general the building is distinctly lacking in the fireplaces and garderobes (toilets) that are the distinguishing feature of castle residential blocks. The answer almost certainly lies under the lawns outside: the surviving building must have been accompanied by other ranges that have now disappeared. The present hall roof is a magnificent oak structure of the early 17th century but is something of a mystery. It may have been built when the castle was leased by the Borough, who intended that the Council of the Welsh Marches should meet there, though there is no evidence that they ever did so, remaining instead at the nearby Council House.

A short distance away from the hall is the postern gate, a small building about which even less is known than the hall. It has a first-floor room over its gateway and a slot for a portcullis; whether one was ever installed is unknown. The postern gate may have been built, or rebuilt, in the 17th century; it formerly (before the railway station was built) gave access to a path down to the river.

The Town Walls

Medieval Shrewsbury was defended by a town wall some 3.2 kilometres long; it encircled the high ground and ran down to the river to enclose and protect the main streets leading from the bridges, Mardol and Wyle Cop. The bridges themselves were also defended: the medieval Welsh Bridge had two gatehouses, one at the Frankwell end and a much larger one in the middle; and the Stone Bridge (the predecessor of English Bridge) had a gatehouse and drawbridge. Additional lengths of town wall ran down St Mary's Water Lane, to provide a defended access way to the river, and from the castle, across Castle Gates and down Meadow Place to the opposite bend of the river, thus providing additional security to the town from the landward side. Two more lengths of wall were built along the riverbank to cover natural fords upstream and downstream of the Welsh Bridge. The town walls were mostly built between c.1220 and 1250 on royal orders, following the successful attack on the town by Welsh forces under Llewellyn. They took many years to complete, and many of the surviving sections show evidence of rebuilding and repair. Surprisingly, except for three or four individual sites, the town wall has never been recorded or surveyed by archaeologists, and the date of construction of many sections remains uncertain.

The medieval town wall along the road of that name. The white (Grinshill) sandstone amongst the generally red-purple Keele Beds sandstone gives an indication of the long history of repairs to the walls

Shrewsbury in the Great Frost. In the winter of 1739 the Severn froze over. This panorama was drawn to commemorate the event, but incidentally provides one of the most detailed views of the medieval town wall and its towers, mostly demolished in the 1790s. The right-hand church is Old St Chad's

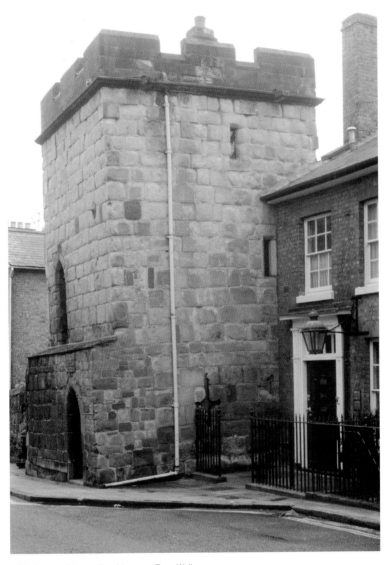

The last surviving medieval tower on Town Walls

Only one mural tower now survives, on Town Walls, and was probably added to the circuit in the mid-14th century; a small section of the wall survives attached to it. Further west along Town Walls and Murivance much of the medieval town wall was demolished at the end of the 18th century when the streets in this area were improved; the site of another mural tower lies directly beneath St Chad's Church, built over it in 1793.

Even less is known about the defences of Anglo-Saxon Shrewsbury. The town was certainly fortified, but the ditches and ramparts that must have existed to protect the town from attack have never been found. But there are clues. Other towns established on river-bound peninsulas (like Bristol, or Lydford in Devon) were defended by a ditch and rampart across the entrance onto the peninsula at its narrowest point. In Shrewsbury, this position is represented by Meadow Place, and the line of the medieval wall, and ditch, that followed it. It may be no coincidence that a tower overlooking the river on this section of wall was known in the 13th century as 'Garewald's tower', or *castellum*. Garewald is an Old English personal name, and may represent a memory of a pre-Conquest town official responsible for this section of the defences (see illustration p.5).

Top: Behind Pride Hill, the lower part of the rear elevation of a hall undercroft of c.1400 (now part of McDonald's) preserves the remains of the 13th-century town wall. The tower is a stair tower belonging to the later hall built on top

Above: The medieval Upper Gate. Its last remnants demolished c.1786, it stood across Castle Gates by the corner of the library buildings (visible in the background)

Left: King's Head Passage, Mardol. The town wall had gone from here by the 1570s but the surveyor stands in the flooded depression left by the old town ditch. The curving plot is much more ancient than the medieval defences that cut across it (see map, p.7)

Below: The face of the 13th-century town wall, found by excavation on Roushill in the late 1950s by Phillip Barker. Medieval documents show that people's rubbish was often tipped in the town ditches close to the gates. The excavation here produced a wealth of discarded pottery, worn-out shoes and other contemporary garbage

The medieval defences of Shrewsbury began to decline in military importance in the 15th century, and in some areas houses were built on top of it. The most spectacular remains of such a house may be found on Pride Hill, in the lower restaurant of McDonald's, which occupies a medieval undercroft - a basement warehouse surviving from a long demolished medieval hall. The back wall can be seen from Raven Meadows; the doorway, windows and the upper two-thirds of the stonework belong to the merchant's undercroft of c.1400, the lower part of the stonework is the levelled remnant of the town wall, built c.1230 with a chamfered plinth along its base.

The town gates were, as in many towns, removed in the 18th and early 19th centuries in response to increasing traffic. Only one survives: the postern (pedestrian) gate at the bottom of St Mary's Water Lane. It is thought to be 13th-century but, like most of the town walls, has never been surveyed. Outside most sections of the wall there was also a town ditch or moat, filled with water from the river wherever possible. This silted up and disappeared centuries ago but has been found by excavation below Murivance, adjoining St Julian's Friars, and behind Mardol, where it was full of contemporary rubbish and preserved organic remains (plants, seeds, leather shoes etc) in the permanently-waterlogged silts. It is still visible as a depression that regularly floods, further down Mardol, behind the King's Head, cutting across the earlier curved riverside plots.

Welsh Bridge and English Bridge

The bridges are the embodiment of Shrewsbury as a border town: Welsh Bridge to the west, English bridge to the east. The predecessors of both bridges were in existence by the 1120s, but at present there is no way of knowing whether they had then just been built or were already ancient.

The medieval Welsh or St George's Bridge. A watercolour of the 1760s, looking north from approximately the site of the present bridge

The present Welsh Bridge was built in 1793-5 about sixty metres downstream from the old medieval bridge it was replacing. The medieval bridge was built in red sandstone, with six main ribbed arches and a flood- or dry-arch at the Frankwell end. It also had two gatehouses. At the west (Frankwell) end was the Welsh or St George's Gate under a square battlemented tower with a guardroom. At the east end stood the Mardol Gate, also under a great tower with machicolated (overhanging) battlements and a classical façade added in the 1530s. The Welsh Gate was taken down in 1773, the Mardol Gate in 1791. The bridge itself was demolished in 1795 but the dry arch was left. In 1935 this last remaining arch was said to be accessible from the cellar of an adjoining house. Today, it survives, neglected but intact, at the rear of a former chapel.

The remains of the medieval Welsh Bridge, standing behind a Victorian chapel in Frankwell. This was the landward or 'dry' arch. It was first noted in the 1930s when it was accessible from the cellar of an adjoining building

It stands only a couple of metres high, below the remains of the ramped bridge approach, but comparison with 18th-century pictures shows that it must continue down below the present ground surface for perhaps another three or four metres, levels having been raised substantially when the Georgian bridge was built.

The present English Bridge was built in 1769-75 to replace a medieval bridge on the same site. The earlier bridge was a much longer and more complex structure, divided into two distinct sections. The main river channel was crossed by the Stone Bridge (a name, incidentally, that suggests that the first Welsh Bridge may have been wooden). The easternmost bridge pier supported the Stone Gate or East Gate, used as a prison, east of which was a drawbridge. The Burghley Map of the 1570s (centrefold) also shows a second, smaller, tower at the Wyle Cop end. What is now Coleham Head, where English Bridge ends, was formerly Coleham Island, there being another (eastern) river channel between it and the Abbey. The second section of the bridge, known as the Monks' Bridge, crossed this eastern channel, which silted up gradually through the Middle Ages and by c.1540 was only navigable in winter. The last major remnant was infilled when the new English Bridge was built; the remains of the old Monks' Bridge still lie beneath the Abbey Foregate roadway outside the Wakeman School, where they were seen and recorded during water-main replacement work in 1999.

But on the town side of the river, still more of the medieval bridge lies buried deep below the bottom of Wyle Cop, where levels have been substantially raised over what was once floodplain. Victorian archaeologists spotted the parapet walls of the bridge in roadworks in 1883 about fifty metres inshore of the present riverbank. And in 2001-2, excavations on St Julian's Friars showed that the

Top: John Gwynn's English Bridge of 1769-75. It was sympathetically rebuilt, wider and lower, in 1925-7 by A W Ward, the Borough Engineer - an early pioneer of conservation in the town

Above: The medieval Stone Bridge, as it survived just before its replacement by the English Bridge. Looking downstream, with the Salop Infirmary in the background, Wyle Cop to the left and Coleham to the right. The masonry bridge shown here was in reality just part of a much longer (thousand-foot) engineering work crossing the floodplain

floodplain once extended right to the bottom of the present gradient, at the junction with Beeches Lane. In short, over a hundred metres of medieval bridge or arched causeway are now thought to lie below this part of Wyle Cop. In total, from the bottom of the Cop to the Abbey, the Stone Bridge and Monks' Bridge together were about 350 metres long, more than three times the length of the present English Bridge.

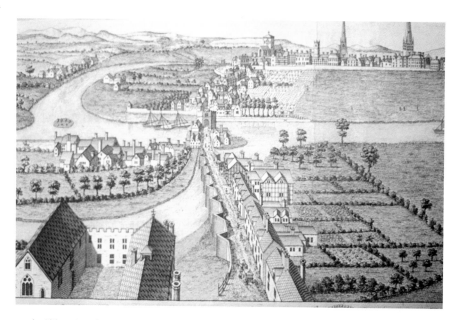

An 18th-century view towards the town from the tower of the abbey church. In the foreground is the medieval Monks' Bridge, the continuation of the Stone Bridge over a second river channel between Coleham Head (formerly Coleham Island) and the Abbey. The remains of the bridge were seen and recorded in 1999 in roadworks along Abbey Foregate, from the English Bridge to the railway viaduct

Two other minor bridges of the medieval town deserve mention. The present Coleham Bridge over the Rea Brook, was built c.1770 to replace a medieval bridge on the same site, first recorded in the early 13th century (and shown on the Burghley Map: see centrefold). There was also a bridge known as the Bagley Bridge, taking Chester Street across the Bagley Brook. This flowed down the west side of Castle Foregate and joined the river where the Gateway Centre now stands. The brook still flows in a culvert beneath the Gateway (its mouth may be seen from the river), and it is said that the medieval bridge across it is still there, below the present roadway.

The Church

It is difficult to overestimate the importance of the Church in the life of the medieval town. The Church dominated the calendar, and the parish was the focus of everyone's spiritual life. Church institutions were powerful landlords in the town and in the surrounding countryside. Church buildings dominated the urban skyline, particularly in an age when private dwellings were of only one or two storeys. Church institutions were major employers of labour, in all the building trades and applied arts, and major consumers of goods and services. Before the Reformation, the town contained four parish churches, the Benedictine Abbey, three friaries, two suburban hospitals, almshouses, and a number of small chapels.

St Mary's

St Mary's Church is also almost certainly the most ancient individual site in the town and is the only one of the great medieval churches within the river loop to have survived intact to the present day. And, as always, there is much more to it than at first appears. St Mary's is a wonderful example of an important church that has been rebuilt and added to over many centuries. The core is a mid-Norman cruciform church of about 1150, represented by the nave, north and south transepts (the arms of the cross) and part of the chancel. The mortar can scarcely have set before the additions began. The present west tower dates to around 1175; the aisles either side of the nave, and the nave arcades, and the lower storey of the south porch, were all added about a generation later, in the years between c.1190 and the early 1200s. In this episode, the Gothic style ('Transitional' and 'Early English') began to creep in: semi-circular arches were rebuilt slightly pointed, both transepts were provided with new, tall, pointed lancet windows, and the chancel was extended eastwards and given a stone-vaulted roof.

There was further work on St Mary's in the 14th century. The original low roofs of the aisles, with a separate gable over each window, were removed and replaced by a much higher single roof; a storey was added to the south porch. And in the years around 1350-1360, just as the town was recovering from the Black Death, a new chapel was built on the south side of the chancel; a century later it was appropriated by the newly founded Drapers' Company, with whom it is still identified. The church was much embellished in the 15th century, the emphasis at the time being on increased verticality. A clerestorey, an extra tier of glazing, was added to the nave, and to the chancel, whose 13th-century vaulted roof had to be removed. The climax of the rebuilding was the addition of the spire to the west tower.

St Mary's church. The tower is late Norman, the spire on top 15th-century

Beneath the church, the churchyard, and the surrounding roads and buildings, lies archaeological evidence of St Mary's early centuries. In 1864, when ducts for the central heating were being excavated, the foundations of what must have been the last Saxon church on the site were seen and recorded. The plan made at the time shows a long building with an apsidal (semi-circular) chancel at the east end. The nave of the Saxon church was found to have been built using stones robbed and re-used from the ruins of Roman Wroxeter, as were the Saxon elements of St Andrew's church, Wroxeter, and St Eata's at Atcham. Although the plan of Saxon St Mary's does not look particularly impressive, it was, for its time, a substantial building. From the ground-plan alone, the Saxon church of St Mary's, Deerhurst, near Tewkesbury, provides a close analogue - and that was,

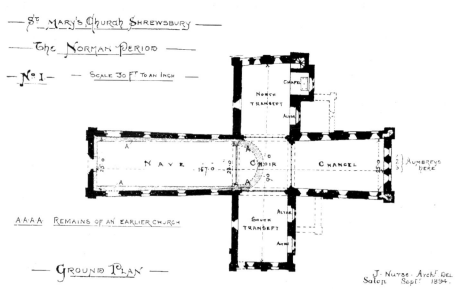

A plan of the Norman parts of the present St Mary's Church, together with the foundations of the Saxon church, discovered in 1864. Except for the semi-circular apse at its eastern end, the Saxon church was built of re-used stone, probably from the ruins of Wroxeter

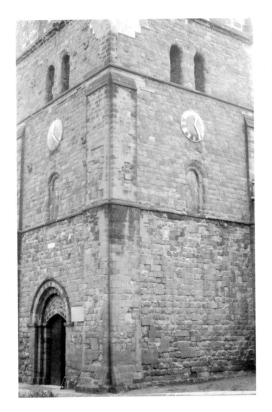

The Norman tower of St Mary's was built c.1175. The stone of the ground-floor storey is probably salvaged Roman masonry from Wroxeter. One huge block at the base of the corner shown here still has the distinctive rectangular slot cut into it for the Roman quarryman's lifting device

pre-Conquest, a large, tall building with two-storey side-chapels and a multi-storey tower. The bottom stage of the present Norman west tower of St Mary's Shrewsbury is also composed of re-used re-dressed Roman masonry, and it may therefore be built out of material salvaged from its Saxon predecessor. The bulk of the former hospital to its east (the old Royal Salop Infirmary, now the Parade) largely conceals St Mary's, apart from its spire, from outside the town. But when first built, on its prominent hilltop site and quite possibly whitewashed externally, it would have been visible for miles around.

Some 11th-century grave slabs and markers kept in the church, decorated in Anglo-Saxon style, are visible relics of the extensive cemetery that lay around the early church. St Mary's then, was not, as it is now, surrounded by roads but lay in a more extensive precinct-like area, with its collegiate buildings around it. As a result, roadworks around the church almost always turn up bones, and sometimes intact burials. The last time this happened was in 1999, during water-main replacement work, when skeletons were found under the roads east and south of the present churchyard.

Old St Chad's

Old St Chad's (so-called to distinguish it from its successor, the present St Chad's, built in 1793) stood in its churchyard at the junction of Princess Street and Belmont/Milk Street. Today, it is the churchyard that survives, along with a small chapel that formerly stood in the angle of the chancel and the south transept of the medieval church. The church itself suffered a calamity in 1788. Early that year cracks had started to appear in one of the four pillars supporting the central tower. The architect to the parish, Thomas Telford, advised that graves, dug too close to the shallow foundations, had weakened the structure, and the tower with its heavy ring of bells needed to be taken down immediately. The parish, however, had other ideas and a mason was employed to cut away the cracked sections and underpin the pillar. Two evenings later, an attempt to ring the bells for a funeral caused the tower to shake so violently that the sexton evacuated the building in a hurry. The following morning, as the clock struck four, half of the tower collapsed, taking the roof of the church with it. The damage was so extensive that the decision was taken to rebuild elsewhere, and to take down the ruins immediately for safety.

Top: The remains of Old St Chad's. Behind, across the High Street valley, can be seen the spires of St Alkmund's and St Mary's

Above: The ruins of St Chad's being cleared after the collapse. Contemporary observers reported that the rubble cores of the walls contained fragments of sculpture from an earlier church on the site

Medieval St Chad's just after the partial collapse of its tower in 1788. The chapel that survives can be seen at the right-hand (east) end

A photograph of the first ever archaeological excavation in Shrewsbury, in 1889 at Old St Chad's.
The trench has exposed the columns that supported the roof of the crypt under the former north transept

The old Saxon minster church of St Chad's had been re-founded and reformed by an early 12th-century bishop of Chester (its patrons after the Conquest), with a staff of ten canons and a dean. The church itself was probably rebuilt in the course of the 12th century as a great cruciform church some 160 feet (c.49 metres) long. The illustrations show that this church, like St Mary's, saw a great deal of rebuilding work in the years around and after 1200. At least the chancel and the surviving south chancel chapel were rebuilt; the aisles may have been added at this time and the transept windows renewed too. The result was a church that looked, from later illustrations of it, to have been built mainly in the early Gothic 'Early English' style. There must have been substantial later alterations too. The illustrations show that, just like the other town churches, the upper parts of its structure were built in a grey-white stone - Grinshill sandstone, characteristic of the later medieval period - contrasting with the red-purple Keele Beds sandstone used in the 12th and 13th centuries. In part at least this may have been a consequence of the disastrous fire in 1393 that happened when a plumber's (lead-worker's) brazier set fire to the roof. The fire spread to neighbouring houses and burnt out much of Wyle Cop - where the after-effects are still evident (see p.60). The workman responsible 'terrified at beholding the sacred edifice in flames endeavoured to escape over the ford of the Severn [from Wyle Cop to Coleham] near the east gate, and was drowned in the attempt'.

After its collapse, the ruins were cleared. The process was watched by two people with a deep interest in the town's history: the Rev. Hugh Owen, author, with the Rev. J B Blakeway, of the 1825 'History of Shrewsbury'; and Henry Pidgeon, a High Street chemist, later Borough Treasurer, and a claim to be regarded as the town's first archaeologist. They both noted early - they thought Saxon - sculptural fragments re-used as rubble in the cores of the medieval walls.

Just outside the crypt the 1889 excavation uncovered this and another burial. Of late Saxon date, the skeletons were enclosed by stone slabs and laid out on beds of charcoal

The site lay open, apart from the surviving chapel, and continued to be used as a graveyard. But in 1889 the newly founded Shropshire Archaeological & Natural History Society sponsored the first-ever excavation in the town, on the site of a crypt that was known to have existed under the north transept. A trench soon located the crypt and the pillars that had supported its vaulted roof, and on its floor the excavators found a bronze cross-headed pin, now known to be a writing stylus of probable 8th- or 9th-century date, almost certainly derived from the early monastery. The stylus (now in Rowley's House Museum) is still the earliest post-Roman artefact ever found in Shrewsbury (see illustration p.3). Beyond the crypt the excavators also found two burials, surrounded by a kerb of stones and laid out on beds of charcoal. Unexpected at the time, this practice is now widely known from the excavation of important late Saxon church sites elsewhere (as at Gloucester and Winchester) and from 19th-century finds outside Shrewsbury Abbey. It appears distinctive of high-status burials, though its meaning is still not certain. The crypt itself was not buried again but remained open until recently and is still only half filled up. Contrary to some accounts it was almost certainly not a Saxon crypt, but a basement or undercroft to provide a level platform for the 12th-century north transept where it stuck out from the slope below the restricted hilltop site of the preceding Saxon church.

A fragment of a carved stone frieze of Saxon (perhaps 9th-century AD) date, built into the cellar wall of a Georgian building on Mardol. It may have come from the ruins of Old St Chad's

What happened to the alleged Saxon sculptural fragments embedded in the medieval wall-cores? Most probably went as hardcore straight into the foundations of the present church. But in the late 1980s an angel's head was reported protruding from the wall of the cellar of a restaurant in Mardol. Investigation a few years later showed that, not only was there indeed an angel's head - part of a medieval capital or vault springing - there were also three blocks of stone bearing an interlace, Stafford-knot type pattern, obviously of Anglo-Saxon style, also incorporated into the masonry walls of the cellar. These fragments proved to be parts of a frieze, a horizontal panel that had once adorned the walls of an important Saxon church. Investigation found that the building, late Georgian brick above ground, had been built, probably in the 1790s, with a stone cellar composed of re-used masonry. We cannot prove where the builder got his stone from, but we can guess.

St Alkmund's and St Julian's

Both churches are listed in Domesday Book, having been founded before the Norman Conquest, but their origins are obscure. St Alkmund's was, according to a tradition preserved by its own priests, founded by Aethelflaed (the 'Lady of the Mercians', wife of Aethelred and daughter of Alfred the Great) in the early 10th century. By 1066 it had twelve houses for its staff of priests. The church is dedicated to the historical figure Ealhmund, a Northumbrian prince murdered c.800AD. A cult was developed around this figure in the 9th century, so it is possible that the church is earlier than its own tradition suggests.

Even less is known of St Julian's (originally St Juliana's) though it was probably a later foundation by one of the late Saxon kings. It may have been founded specifically for the first residents of Wyle Cop, a street now known to have been occupied before the Norman Conquest following the discovery of its rubbish-dump at the bottom of the hill. St Julian(a)'s overlooked the street from its hilltop site, and its medieval parish exactly covered the street and the properties either side of it.

Both St Alkmund's and St Juliana's were rebuilt before c.1200 in the Norman style. St Alkmund's is said to have had nave arcades of round arches resting on round pillars; it was a cruciform church, with north and south transepts. 18th-century illustrations suggest that, as at St Mary's, new pointed Gothic windows were introduced around or after 1200. Having been an important church with a collegiate staff of twelve, it was gradually 'asset-stripped' and its possessions given to the new abbey at Lilleshall; thereafter, it was an ordinary parish church. But this is not to suggest that it was poverty-stricken: like many urban churches, it continued to grow organically by piecemeal additions.

All that now survives above ground is the west tower, added at the end of the 15th century. The remainder of the medieval church was demolished in 1794: the roof was in need of repair, but the parish feared that the old rambling building was unsound, and might, like St Chad's, collapse without warning.

Because St Julian's was rebuilt relatively early, in 1748-9, even less is known about its medieval form, apart from the surviving early 13th-century west tower. Its solid-looking stepped construction is assumed to be a response to the difficulties of building on a soft sandy hillside. St Juliana's was not a cruciform church like the others: its plan

St Alkmund's (foreground) and St Julian's, formerly St Juliana's, on their hilltop site. Both had been Saxon minster churches; the King's Market lay around them. St Alkmund's parish included the wealthiest core of the town centre

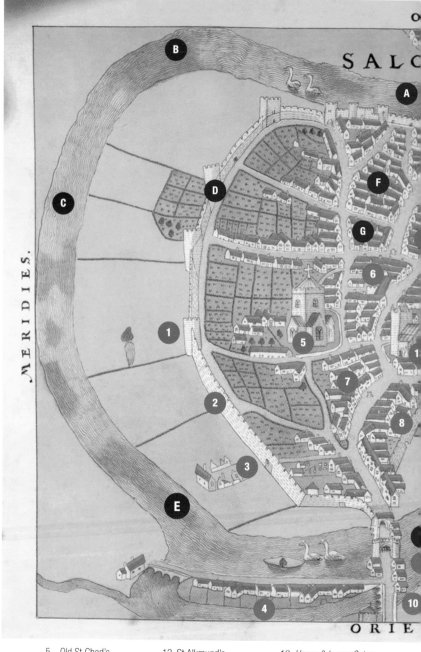

SALO

MERIDIES.

ORIE

 Historic
Landmarks

1 Town Walls tower
2 Town Walls
3 St Julian's/Greyfriars
4 Coleham Island

5 Old St Chad's
6 THE SQUARE
7 Henry Tudor House
8 Nag's Head, Wyle Cop
9 *The Stone Bridge*
10 *The Monk's Bridge*
11 Bennett's Hall

12 St Alkmund's
13 St Julian(a)'s
14 ST MARY'S
15 *Blackfriars*
16 St Mary's Water Lane
17 The Council House
18 Meadow Place wall

19 *Upper & Lower Gates*
20 THE CASTLE
21 Coton Hill

Sites in italics -
no visible remains

36

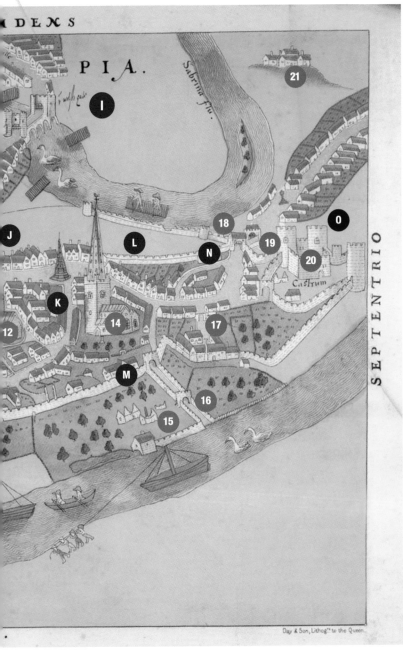

DE XS

PIA.

Sabrina Flu.

SEPTENTRIO

Castrum

Day & Son, Lithog. to the Queen.

Modern
Landmarks

A   Welsh Bridge
B   Suspension bridge (foot)
C   Kingsland Bridge
D   St Chad's Church

E   Greyfriars Bridge (foot)
F   Rowleys House Museum
G   Market Hall
H   English Bridge
I   Council Office
    (Frankwell)

J   Pride Hill
    Shopping Centre
K   Post Office
L   Charles Darwin
    ShoppingCentre
M   The Parade (ex RSI)

N   The Library
O   Railway Station

was simpler, though side aisles flanked its nave by c.1200. Early 18th-century illustrations suggest that the south aisle and the Shearmen's Chapel on the north side of the chancel were rebuilt in the later Middle Ages in the Perpendicular style. The present upper storey was added to the west tower probably in the early 16th century.

Medieval St Alkmund's, as seen from Bear Steps. Only the tower survived the rebuilding of the church in 1794

St Julian(a)'s church. The 13th- and 16th-century tower surviving at the west end of Thomas Farnoll Pritchard's nave of 1749-50. Its parish extended down Wyle Cop

Chapels

As well as the four parish churches, medieval Shrewsbury had a number of small chapels, all but one of which have long gone. There were two chapels associated with the castle. St Michael's stood in the inner bailey, was in ruins by the end of the Middle Ages, and may be the roofless ruin shown in the castle by the Burghley Map of c.1575 (see centrefold). The inhabitants of the castle's outer bailey had the chapel of St Nicholas, a simple Norman building that stood on Castle Street close to the gateway to the Council House. It was demolished and replaced in 1868 and its successor, a tall Victorian neo-Norman building, is currently in use as an office.

The medieval chapel of St Nicholas, on Castle Gates, built to serve the castle's Outer Bailey. It was replaced in 1868. From Owen & Blakeway's 1825 History of Shrewsbury

There was a chapel of St Martin, served by priests from St Alkmund's, about halfway up Grope Lane; it was probably there by c.1100. By the 1220s there was a chapel and cemetery of St Werburgh, behind the houses on the east side of Swan Hill, just north of Swan Hill Court (once a much longer lane). Finally, there was a chapel of St Romald, also with a cemetery, on the east side of Barker Street, within the area of the present car park on the north side of Rowley's House Museum; this is discussed later in the context of the Romaldesham district.

The 1868 St Nicholas's chapel, now offices.
To the right is the timber-framed gatehouse
of the Council House, whose buildings
accommodated the Council of the Welsh
Marches in the 16th and 17th centuries

Shrewsbury Abbey

Shrewsbury Abbey (described in detail elsewhere: see Further Reading) was a Norman foundation of the 1080s by Earl Roger of Montgomery on the site of a wealthy pre-Conquest suburban household with its own private chapel. The site on which it was founded was also a riverside site, at the junction of the Rea Brook with the old eastern channel of the River Severn. This gradually silted up through the later Middle Ages, but still reappears in the more serious floods.

The Benedictine Abbey was, on a national scale, a very small one, though in local terms the 70-metre long Norman Abbey church was nearly three times the size of the Saxon St Mary's. The cloisters lay south of the Abbey church; to the west, a large courtyard was developed that came to house the buildings necessary to the Abbey in its dealings with the outside world. Guest accommodation for Abbey visitors and probably pilgrims was an important element of this, and a unique range of structures was built along the Abbey's waterfront. Parts of this range still survive, and have been known since the

Shrewsbury Abbey, in the floods of November
2000, when the old eastern channel of the
Severn between the church and Coleham
Head re-appeared

19th century as the 'Old Infirmary'. The building at the south end of the range had a hall (probably a guest hall) and a private chamber at first-floor level with what appears to have been a water-gate, probably accessed from a dock or slip-way, below. In the 15th century a long range was built next to it with a series of arched doorways along the waterfront. The use of this building is less certain, but could similarly have provided for the movement of goods and people coming by river in its lower storey, with some kind of accommodation above. There may have been another first-floor hall at the north end of the range, but as this was entirely demolished in 1836 little is known of it.

As the Abbey developed it became desperate for space along its south side, where most of its domestic ranges were located; to the south lay the old course of the Rea Brook, a watermill, and the Rea floodplain. Excavations in the 1980s showed that the abbey created room for its buildings by reclamation on the floodplain edge. The landfill dumped in the process was found to seal permanently waterlogged deposits containing a goldmine of well preserved archaeological finds, including food wastes and plant remains, discarded pottery and shoes. Some late medieval abbots were generous hosts, and this is amply borne out by archaeological evidence of rich foods and feasting in the guest houses of this part of the precinct. The shoe-soles discarded by a cobbler in a late medieval latrine showed that both men and women were present here, outside the cloister. The most remarkable individual find was a silver bowl or saucer, used to contain sauces or custard at the dinner table, stamped with a leopard's head, the earliest English hall-mark ever discovered

For all its qualities as a buried archaeological site, Shrewsbury Abbey is not equally well preserved above ground. The monastic church lost its east end, central tower and transepts when the Abbey was dissolved by Henry VIII's commissioners in 1540; most of the cloister ranges went at the same time. One part that did survive was the reader's pulpit, formerly an integral part of the monks' refectory hall, used for reading from the scriptures during the otherwise silent communal meals. The pulpit was probably saved by the first lay owners of the site after the Dissolution. It stood in their garden, overlooked by a gallery in a newly built timber-framed range attached to the former abbot's house. Other parts of the site were colonised by industry, one of the owners developing a tanning business on the site of the former guests' kitchen. Water-milling continued on the site well into the 19th century, and the last Abbey Mill (built c.1800) finally burnt down in 1906. Thomas Telford's new road cut through the remains of the cloisters in 1836, the last remains of the precinct wall were torn down in the 1840s, and the coming of the railways in the 1850s and 60s resulted in further demolitions. The remains of the 'Old Infirmary' are in the care of the Shropshire Wildlife Trust, and are open to visitors. The river channel outside is now a main road.

The Friaries

Like every medieval town of any size or importance, Shrewsbury became a magnet for the mendicant orders in the 13th century. The friars sought a simpler version of monastic life, but one that was dedicated to preaching: they therefore sought out centres of population. But as they were late arrivals to the well-developed towns, their patrons usually found sites for new friaries outside the town walls. Such was the case in Shrewsbury, where three friaries were founded on riverside sites. The Dominican Friars (Black Friars) established their precinct outside the town wall below St Mary's; the Franciscans (Grey Friars) built their precinct on a great reclamation platform in the floodplain south of Wyle Cop (St Julian's Friars); the Augustinian or Austin Friars were given a site outside the town ditch below the Welsh Bridge, in the area of the Sixth Form College.

Little is known of any of these sites. The Blackfriars precinct was established on hillside terraces, and test-trenches dug before housing was built there showed that nearly all below-ground remains had been thoroughly destroyed previously. Some remains do however survive on the bottom terrace level, by the river at the bottom of Water Lane. Excavations in the 1820s and in the 1970s found burials, the remains of the friary church (which was enormous) and the basements of one range of the cloister buildings. The Greyfriars site has been sampled by test-trenches around the periphery, but the core of the precinct is unexplored. One range of buildings survives in use along the riverbank. Remains of the Augustinian Friary were found just below the surface by archaeological test trenches in the early 1990s, but this part of the site appears to have been destroyed by subsequent redevelopment. The last surviving friary building - a mysterious tower-like stone building by the river - was demolished in the 1940s. More remains are to be expected below the college buildings, and building work occasionally reveals burials from the friary cemetery.

Above: Until its demolition in 1941 this was the last surviving building of the Augustinian or Austin Friary, though its original function is not known. A riverside restaurant and nightclub now occupy its site. From Owen & Blakeway's 1825 History of Shrewsbury

Right: The only surviving building of the Franciscan Friary (the Greyfriars or St Julian's Friars). It was not part of the friars' cloister but lay on the edge of their precinct, right by the river on top of a massive retaining wall. All three friaries were founded when the medieval town was nearly fully-grown and adopted riverside sites outside the town walls

The Square

The Square is generally regarded as the centre of the historic town: the Old Market Hall of 1596, the early 19th-century Music Hall and a number of the finest 16th-century timber-framed houses all emphasise the great significance to the town of this public open space. But, within reach of recorded history, it was a marginal, wild place, used as a place of punishment.

A 'kettle-hole' in its natural state outside the town at Weeping Cross. The Square in the town centre was a market place created by infilling just such a depression, once filled with water and sediment and used as a place of punishment

The Square as we know it was officially established as a new market place in 1261, the old King's Market on the hill top between St Alkmund's and St Juliana's having become too small to cope with the growing urban economy. But some kind of market had been there since before the 1220s, and documents record the presence of selds - stalls, or groups of stalls in small shopping arcades - by the 1240s. The area was already partly built up, but where the Square now stands was a natural water-filled, peat-fringed hollow, of the type known to geologists as a kettle-hole and common throughout the countryside around Shrewsbury. The name of this hollow was the Gumbestolesmore, a name last heard of around 1245. It means the gumble-stool mere - the ducking stool marsh. This device was used as a punishment for scolds, and for bakers and brewers who contravened trading regulations. But punishment (even human sacrifice) in water and bog was a tradition

A local ducking-stool or Gumblestool. This one is preserved in Leominster Church, and was used as late as the beginning of the 19th century

extending back into prehistory. So it is just possible that this valley-bottom place, on the parish boundary between the two oldest Anglo-Saxon minster churches, St Mary's and St Chad's, had a much longer and more sinister history than its use for the enforcement of trading regulations once the area was built up.

The documentary evidence for the creation of the Square as a market place is quite limited. It records the fact of its creation in 1261, the paving of the High Street in 1269-70, and the employment of carpenters in September 1270 to start work on a new town Guildhall across the end of the new market. Nothing was recorded of any reclamation scheme to fill-in Gumbestolesmore, but such a scheme certainly took place, and on a vast scale. The former existence of the pool or mere in or next to the Square first became apparent in 1783 when a new Shirehall was constructed to replace the medieval Guildhall or Boothall. The Shirehall was built where the much-reviled Princess House now stands, on the east side of the Square. The workmen dug down nineteen feet through 'a great deposit of something like manure' including a layer of 'grain, straw, dung of cattle, and nut-shells' without finding solid ground. The foundations were laid in this material, on wooden beams. Not surprisingly, they failed within fifty years and the Shirehall had to be completely rebuilt in 1832-34. Smirke, the architect of the new building, did not make the same mistake: his men excavated another ten feet down to find solid ground and lay solid concrete foundations. An extension to the Shirehall was built in 1881 and the same waterlogged deposit was seen again. It contained the bones of 'stag, fallow deer, roebuck, goat, ox, sheep, wild boar and large fowl' and fifteen feet down a row of oak piles was found along the edge of the High Street. Building work further east in the 1920s found more peat bog; even Clive's Statue in the Square, erected in 1860, had to be built on a concrete raft to stop it sinking.

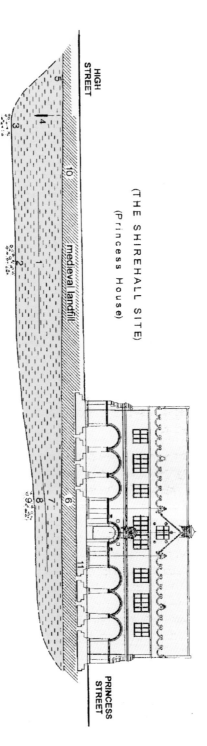

**HIGH
STREET**

(THE SHIREHALL SITE)

(Princess House)

medieval landfill

THE SQUARE

Archaeological section through
kettle-hole/pond deposits
(medieval *Gumbestolesmore*)

1. **Level of 1783 Shirehall foundations** (~ 5.7m)

2. **Level of 1832 Shirehall foundations** (~ 8.8m)

3. 1881 Shirehall extension, natural ground probed at ~ 9.1m

4. 1881 Shirehall extension, preserved oak piles along street edge

5. 1999 Water-main **watching-brief**, 'peat' at ~ 2.1m under sand

6. Redeposited sands/gravels to ~ 3.3m

7. **Black waterlogged silts**

8. Grey waterlogged clay-silt

9. **Natural gravel at** ~ 6.9m

10. 2003 power supply point, redeposited sands/gravels to ~1.6m

2001 Old Market Hall **watching-brief and borehole, west transept**

11. 2003 OMH watching-brief, **east transept**

**PRINCESS
STREET**

An archaeological cross-section of the Square and the Market Hall. It shows the ten-foot thick layer of sands and gravels tipped in the medieval period to reclaim the former pond, the wide foundations supporting the 1596 Market Hall on this material and the depth of peat and sediments still buried beneath

The full extent of the old Gumbestolesmore and its black, wet deposits was not appreciated until work began on the restoration of the Old Market Hall in 2000. Suspicions were first aroused by the discovery that its foundations rested, not on natural ground, but on re-deposited, mixed up, sands, gravels and clays. What lay beneath? The answer was provided by a deep borehole for a hydraulic lift-piston. Below lay black pond mud, turning gradually grey with depth until natural gravel was reached seven metres (23 feet) below the pavement. Between the surface and the top of the mud was a depth of three metres (10 feet) of re-deposited natural material - a medieval landfill deposit, dumped to fill in the mere and allow the Square to be laid out. This deposit has since been seen elsewhere under the paving in the Square, and it is clear that to create the new market place around six thousand cubic metres of landfill was tipped first. The source of this material was probably the hillside below Fish Street and Butcher Row. There is no slope there now (apart from Grope Lane): the shops on that side of the High Street run back level to retaining walls supporting the higher ground. This terracing was also a creation of the medieval period, and the red sandstone retaining walls were, in the 19th century, mistaken for a lost section of town wall (see p.53). The terrace accommodated at least one substantial mansion, belonging to a wealthy 13th-century merchant family. The excavation into the hillside would have yielded around twelve thousand cubic metres of natural material - more than enough for the infilling of the valley bottom, and it may well be that reclamation of the Gumbestolesmore and the terracing of the valley slopes were conceived as a single project. Aside from the defences, The Square may represent the first major civil engineering project undertaken by the growing town.

The Old Market Hall was built in 1596 to replace earlier timber buildings on the site. The builders obviously knew what they were about. The new foundations were cut only a metre deep into the landfill to avoid penetrating into the mud below, but were up to 2.3 metres (7.5 feet) wide to spread the load - with complete success, there is no sign of subsidence four centuries later. It was built with 'a hall aloft and a large market house for corn beneath'. The first-floor hall was rented from the Corporation by the Drapers' Company, who held their Thursday flannel market there.

One other long-forgotten aspect of Shrewsbury's medieval market place provides an exceptionally vivid illustration of how town life has changed over the centuries. Leading down the hill towards the Square from the old King's Market is Grope Lane, one of the town's most picturesque streets. Its name reflects the fact that it was, in the Middle Ages, a place

Gullet Passage, looking towards the Square, up the steps onto the medieval reclamation platform over the former pond

The Market Hall of 1596

of prostitution. Once, many English medieval towns had a Grope Lane, and in almost every case they were later re-named - York's became Grape Lane; Gropecuntelane in Wells, Somerset, became Grope, then Grove Lane. Shrewsbury's was last referred to as Gropecountelane in 1561, but even in its reduced form (and still without an official street sign) it is a very rare survivor. Crucially, nearly every known Grope Lane led directly off each town's market place or its High Street; in two places (Worcester and Newcastle) they were associated with public quays. The implication is that such streets were used for rendezvous in the open air, close to the markets, either for the benefit of country-folk on market days or because (as a historian of London's Cheapside put it) the opportunity was taken to widen the scope of transactions with women traders. It is a reminder that medieval towns were about more than the historian's traditional concerns of power, economics, defence and religion.

The houses
and shops of
the medieval town

The ancestors of Shrewsbury's timber buildings

Pre-Conquest Shrewsbury is likely to have been built up with mostly one- and some two-storey buildings supported by timber posts dug into the ground. Most towns of this period had buildings built over rectangular timber-lined cellars used for craft-working and storage, although none of these has yet come to light in Shrewsbury. Only one pre-Conquest house has so far been excavated. This was found by a Birmingham University team set back behind the corner of Pride Hill and the High Street during the redevelopment of the old Owen Owen department store. Post- and stake-holes for the walls framed an area of burnt or sooty clay, representing the floor.

The clay floor and the stake holes of the walls of a Saxon house excavated near the corner of Pride Hill and the High Street

A building of similar design but three centuries later in date was excavated by a local archaeological team behind the Plough, between Mardol Head and the Square, in the early 1970s. The timber posts and stakes of its walls were preserved in the wet, peaty soil. Inside was a central hearth on a bed of clay; outside was a wooden trough, thought to have been used for some industrial process.

The earliest surviving houses

Shrewsbury can boast a group of medieval town houses that are amongst the earliest survivors in the country, dating between c.1250 and c.1300. The earliest of all is also the most unusual. This is the fragment of a sandstone building known as Bennett's Hall, incorporated into a modern shop at no.2 Pride Hill. As you walk off the street into the shop a wall of red sandstone faces you with a fireplace set centrally between the remains of two arched openings. These are slightly above the main floor level; below them at basement level is a second pair of arches.

Bennett's Hall on Pride Hill, exposed during redevelopment in 1959-60 when the remains of the cross-wall with its fireplace and doorways were incorporated into a new shop. Built c.1250-60, this is the town's earliest partly surviving house, visible in the shop next to Lloyd's Bank

The remains are those of a cross- or partition wall that once stood within a large medieval hall, running back at right angles to the street, its street end cut into the natural hillside. The fireplace heated a fine, private room at the street end; at the back, beyond the cross-wall, was a slightly larger room, thought to have been an open-roofed hall. Photographs and records made c.1959-60 during the construction of the modern shop show that a blind arcade - a series of shallow arches - ran around the inside of the walls, possibly of both rooms. Below, level with the yard behind the building, was an undercroft, used for warehousing and storage. Recent historical research suggests that this large, ornate and unusual building belonged to the de Ludlow family - builders of Stokesay Castle and among the country's leading wool exporters; its date suggests it may have been built for Nicholas de Ludlow, one of the greatest of the English merchants of the 13th century.

Vaughan's Mansion. An early 19th-century view of the hall standing at the back of its courtyard off Market Street. It was built c.1280-90 for a leading merchant and survives in part within the Music Hall

The remains of another wealthy mansion of the period survive incorporated into the Music Hall, fronting the Square and Market Street. This is Vaughan's Mansion, probably built c.1270-1280 for William Vaughan, another leading wool exporter and a member of one of the town's wealthiest mercantile families. Again, the hall is cut into a hillside, with the main living space at first-floor level (in relation to Market Street) over an undercroft. At the time of writing, the hall is in use as a bar and the undercroft as a cinema. The medieval building's service wing and an ornate timber porch (see picture) were demolished to make room for the Music Hall, opened in 1840. Inside the hall, the present timber hammer-beam roof was built following a fire in 1917 but copies the late medieval roof that was damaged. Some of the original 13th-century rectangular stone windows, though blocked, survive and are displayed within the present building.

The Hole-in-the Wall pub on Shoplatch contains the remains of another great stone building, possibly belonging to the Schitte family, documented as holding property in the area in the 13th century. The building originally extended from the street frontage back along what is now Drayton's Passage. The mutilated remains of its main door still provide the main entrance to the pub from the passage. Inside are the remains of blocked windows and other features at ground and first-floor levels; there are further remains in the cellars of the adjacent premises on Shoplatch. When the building was renovated by the brewery in the 1980s a series of sharply-pointed arches were found in its wall footings. These (no longer visible) were relieving arches to strengthen the foundations, the underlying ground being wet and soft, adjacent to a former stream and peat bog (see p.11).

There were other great stone mansions in the 13th- and 14th-century town: some survive as fragments, others have gone completely. Grandest of all was Charlton Hall, which lay next to Vaughan's Mansion in the street block between Market Street, Swan Hill and St John's Hill. Early 19th-century drawings and contemporary documents record the existence of a large 13th-century ground-floor hall next to a three-storey 14th-century chamber block, said in 1808 to be 100 feet long, which would have contained the more private apartments. This was, in the 14th century, the town house of the Charltons, a county gentry family active in court circles. In 1325 John de Charlton, Lord of Powys and a major landowner in the region, was granted a Licence to Crenellate, allowing him to build a fortified precinct wall around the site, thus turning it into something like a fortified urban manor house. The hall was demolished in 1823; the chamber block is said to have been converted into a theatre in 1765 but, ruinous in the 1820s, it was demolished c.1833 for the new Theatre Royal. This building survives as a discount shop; a glance at its back wall reveals courses of re-used sandstone masonry, almost certainly all that now remains above ground of the old Charlton Hall buildings.

Fragments of many other wealthy stone buildings survive, usually trapped in the cellars of much later buildings (see chapter on Underground Shrewsbury), and recent historical research has been able to identify many of them, and their owners/builders. The remains of one, for example, were recently rediscovered incorporated into 18th-century buildings, their cellars and back yards, on the High Street. These remains (in the area of 10-11 High Street and to the rear of the Three Fishes pub on Fish Street) were identified by historians as those of Burgh Hall, named after their late medieval owner, Sir John Burgh. But the hall had probably been built much earlier, by the super-rich Stury family in the 13th century. At the end of the Middle Ages the site was sub-divided and most of its buildings adapted or demolished over the next two centuries. The remains today are fragmentary, divided between several modern properties and partly concealed behind plaster at ground- and first-floor level in the High Street buildings.

Top: One of the buildings of Charlton Hall, which lay between Shoplatch and Swan Hill. Built in the 13th and 14th centuries, it was once surrounded by a crenellated wall, giving it the appearance of a fortified manor house set in the county town

Above: Fragments of sandstone walls behind the frontages of High Street and Fish Street represent the remains of another lost medieval mansion - Burgh's Hall. It was a two-level building (like Vaughan's Mansion) terraced into the slope above the High Street

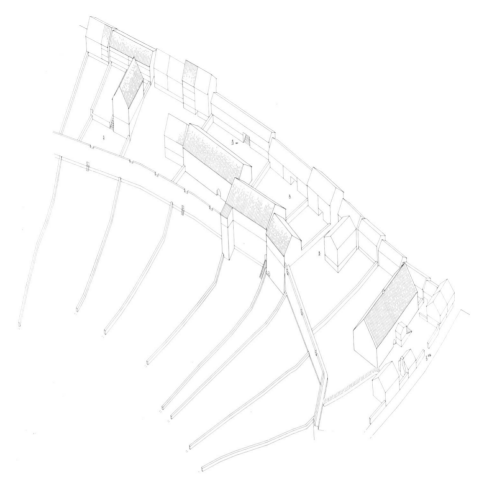

An archaeological reconstruction of medieval buildings in their plots along the north-west side of Pride Hill. Bennett's Hall is in the foreground, the McDonald's building with its stair tower halfway along. The street frontage was lined with shops; the merchants' halls usually lay behind, some built on the medieval town wall. Buildings with shaded roofs - good evidence; unshaded roofs - hypothetical

A Victorian sketch shows the sandstone walls in the back yards with medieval doorways or windows at two levels (the lower, High Street, and upper, Fish Street level) suggesting that the building was once very similar to Vaughan's Mansion on the opposite side of the High Street valley, terraced into the slope, with upper-level living accommodation.

Surveys of the cellars of the shops on the north-west side of Pride Hill have also revealed a distinctive medieval pattern of building there. Away from the street frontage, terraced into the hillside below the shops are the remains of a number of sandstone-built undercrofts; the halls that once stood on top of them are long gone; the McDonald's restaurant site is the best known and most accessible. Very few medieval building remains are known from the street frontage, though documents reveal that, just as today, it was lined with shops, usually with living-accommodation above, in the form of rooms referred to as chambers or solars. So, from archaeological survey and historical research it has been possible to resurrect in outline the general appearance of this part of the street.

Large stone or stone and timber-framed halls lay tucked away behind the frontage, often at the back of a courtyard. The latter would have been accessed via an entry off the frontage. The halls generally lay across the width of very wide plots that ran from the street back down the slope to the meadows below or to a path at the foot of the slope (now Raven Meadows), and provided scope for grazing and watering livestock. On the street itself were shops, often in rows of four or more. They were two-storey buildings, at least until the 15th century when three storeys became common in the main streets.

Timber buildings

Bear Steps. The late 14th-century hall is on the right. It was probably a parish guild hall

Only three timber-framed buildings survive that are near-contemporaries of the sandstone halls of the 'super-rich' families of the decades either side of 1300. The earliest is at 12-12a Fish Street, at the end of Butcher Row. The brick exterior conceals a timber-framed building dated by dendrochronology to 1358-9. It formerly had an elaborate jettied (overhanging) façade onto St Alkmund's churchyard, but this was concealed soon after as the Bear Steps hall was built right up against it. The Bear Steps hall may possibly have been built as a parish guild hall, around 1384, historical research having found a document complaining about the non-arrival of a delivery of timber to the Guild of the Holy Cross, of St Alkmund's.

Also from the mid-14th century is a timber hall encapsulated within the Old Mansion, St Mary's Street, now taken into the Prince Rupert Hotel. Tree-ring dating shows that the two-bay hall, which stands on a sandstone undercroft that appears to be even older, was built in 1366. In its roof timbers are traces of a smoke louvre that would have allowed smoke to escape from the central hearth burning in the middle of the floor below.

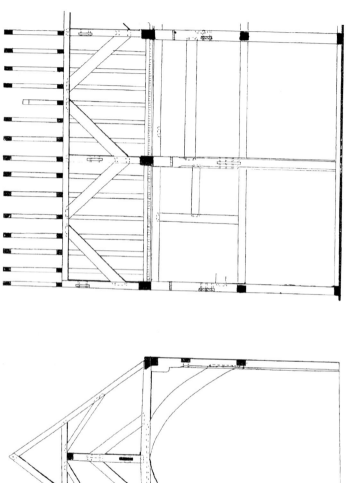

A cross-section through the timber frame of the hall of the Old Mansion, off St Mary's Street, tree-ring dated to 1366. A sandstone cellar or undercroft beneath it is even older. The building is now part of the Prince Rupert Hotel

0 2m

Looking down on Fish Street from the tower of St Julian's. The nearer buildings are medieval, built to a double-range design of shops with living accommodation over along the frontage and open roofed halls behind

Many more timber buildings survive from the 15th century (about thirty-two, a remarkable total). One building type of which there are a number of examples is related to the pattern of development found on Pride Hill, with shops on the frontage and halls behind, built across the width of the plot. The timber-framed buildings at the St Julian's end of Fish Street are built in this way, the rear halls joined to the back walls of the frontage shops.

The building at the head of Compasses Passage on Wyle Cop is of the same type, and yet another, more elaborate, example has been found concealed behind the brick façade at 12-14 Mardol. There, an open hall at first-floor level is attached to the rear of a row of three-storey timber-framed and jettied shops. Across Wyle Cop from Compasses Passage, the Nags Head is another early 15th-century jettied building; the remains of its hall, in the pub garden behind, have been dated to c.1420. All that is now left of the hall is its 'lower end': its cross-passage with a gallery above, and a private chamber over a service room (perhaps a buttery or pantry). The open-roofed medieval hall itself was demolished in the 1950s, as it was becoming unstable and threatening a bicycle repair business in an adjacent corrugated iron shed.

The remains of the ornate timber-framed hall, surviving at the rear of the Nag's Head on Wyle Cop

57

The famous Abbot's House on Butcher Row. A row of shops with accommodation above, it was built as a speculative investment for Lilleshall Abbey in 1457-9, its original shop fronts are some of the best preserved examples in England

In one way the buildings of five hundred years ago show themselves to be the product of a very developed, almost modern, property market. Row buildings - terraces of multiple units built speculatively for rent - are one of the most common forms of building. The properties already described on Fish Street, Mardol or on Pride Hill with two, three or four shops on a plot frontage are one variant of this. Another is the free-standing row building, of which the most famous example is the Abbot's House on Butcher Row. This was built between 1457 and 1459 as a speculative investment by the Abbey of Lilleshall, and provides a series of shops along Butcher Row, and around the corner into Fish Street (where the building has been truncated). There was accommodation on two levels above the shops. The shop-fronts are amongst the best preserved medieval examples in England. The arched openings of the shops are now of course glazed, but would originally have been closed only by a 'stall-board', a large shutter, hinged at the bottom, that would be let down in daytime into the horizontal position to serve as a counter, suspended by ropes or chains. The customer generally stood in the street; the shops themselves functioned more as workshops and storage and display-space than as retailing space as such.

The Henry Tudor House on Wyle Cop, built by a wealthy brewer in 1430

Another stupendous row building is Mytton's Mansion on Wyle Cop, just possibly built by Reginald Mytton in 1406, in which year a document records a complaint that he was allegedly blocking the street with trees. The original shop fronts along the street have all been replaced, but more survive up the entry passage through to the rear of the premises: suggesting an entrepreneurial concern to extract the maximum possible retail value from the site. Something similar may be seen in the courtyard of the Old Post Office, behind 2-3 Milk Street, where restoration work in the 1990s uncovered another, later 15th-century, shop front in what seems like a very unpromising situation for passing trade.

Mytton's Mansion was probably built in the aftermath of the 1393 fire that started at Old St Chad's (see p.33). The other early 15th-century buildings on the street may all belong to the post-fire rebuilding, including Henry Tudor house, just up the hill from Mytton's Mansion. This is now known to have been built by Nicholas Clement, a wealthy brewer. The frontage range (dendro-dated to 1430-31) has a hall and private chamber on the first floor, above shops and the entry to Barracks Passage; above the hall on the second floor is a further pair of rooms with open timber roofs. Behind, running back down the plot, stands a long jettied range dated to 1426 and thought to have been a malt house. This building, together with the frontage range and another medieval timber-framed building encased in the brickwork of the restaurant on the opposite side of the passage, forms one of the best preserved built-up medieval plots in any English town.

The houses
and shops of
the Tudor town

From the 1560s on, new timber-framed houses were given a new decorative treatment that, although medieval in inspiration, marked a transition to Elizabethan tastes with marked Renaissance overtones. So distinctive is this style that it has become known as the 'Shrewsbury school of carpentry'. Its characteristics were S-shaped curved braces; twisted 'cable mouldings' running up the principal posts often terminating with grotesque heads or small fluted capitals; elaborately-carved tie-beams and barge boards on the gables, sometimes bearing the owner's initials and date; and fancy finials. Timber-frame panels were infilled with close studding (close-set non-structural vertical timbers); diagonal and herringbone studs, and studs with sunken quatrefoil decorations.

The earliest building in town known to have been built in this style was the (now-demolished) Lloyd's Mansion, built in 1570 on the corner of the Square and Princess Street, though the style can be taken back to c.1550 in the work by the master carpenter John Sandford at Pitchford Hall. Behind their facades, post-1560 Shrewsbury buildings also show a mixture of the old and the new in their internal planning. The pairing of the medieval hall, the one principal heated room, with a smaller and more private chamber, was still present. But in new buildings the hall now had a flat ceiling and no longer an open timber roof, and the room was given less prominence in the plan. Overall, houses now had more, smaller, rooms, affording a greater degree

Timber-framing characteristic of Tudor
Shrewsbury on two adjacent late 16th -
century High Street houses

of privacy. New fireplaces and chimneys were being added to old buildings, and new floors were introduced across former open halls. Accommodation at attic level was increasing, and was particularly used for live-in servants and staff, present in perhaps 40% of town-centre households. As before, most of the buildings that survive were built by the urban elite; in the 16th century this usually meant the wealthier drapers (members of the Drapers' Company), and lawyers.

The outstanding example of a private building of this period is probably Ireland's Mansion, the tallest surviving timber-frame in town, at the end of the High Street. This was built c.1560 for the Ireland family, probably for Robert Ireland junior, a merchant and a member of the Mercers' Company, active in the Welsh cloth trade. It has a frontage range of three storeys plus attics and stone cellars, and a substantial rear wing. The close-studded façade is symmetrical with projecting octagonal bays rising through the first and second floors flanking projecting rectangular bays. At roof level are four projecting dormer gables with tie-beams and collar-beams decorated with carved intertwined vines. It is jettied out on two levels. The symmetrical façade does not quite fit with the planning of the interior, which was divided between three separate tenements. The central tenement was the largest, for the family's occupation. At ground level a passage ran down the side of a shop to give access to a back room and stairs to the upper floors. On the first floor there was probably one very large room on the frontage with a smaller room behind. This arrangement, repeated on the floor above, can be seen as an echo of the medieval hall and chamber arrangement. Above were attics. Either side were two smaller, but still substantial, tenements for rent. Ireland's Mansion is not just a wealthy family's town house - it is a substantial exercise in speculative commercial property.

No.16 High Street, built for a wealthy draper and alderman in the late 16th century. It stands on the corner of the notorious Grope Lane, a unique survival of the street life of the medieval town

On the opposite side of the High Street, on the corner of Grope Lane, stands another house of the period, smaller, but nevertheless the house of a very wealthy individual. This is 16 High Street (formerly the Cross Keys), a timber-framed house built by William Jones, a draper, alderman and

Rowley's House, Barker Street. This building was probably that described in 1635 as a 'vast great brewhouse'. The principal range (right) was preserved as the Shrewsbury Museum & Art Gallery; the other ranges were demolished c.1930 for the creation of the town's first municipal car park

four times town bailiff. This too is classic 'Shrewsbury school of carpentry' externally, with a strong flavour of medieval planning lingering inside. The principal rooms are similarly on the first floor, the most important being at the front. This room, the hall equivalent, has a flat plaster ceiling divided into compartments by timber beams. The fireplace was at the east end of this room, opposite the projecting bay window of the two-storey porch; it seems this was considered the 'high' end of the building, heated and lit by the equivalent of a bay or oriel window.

There are more than two hundred buildings of the 16th and 17th centuries surviving in Shrewsbury and the interested reader will find better and more comprehensive accounts elsewhere than is possible in this short book (see Further Reading). It would however be wrong to leave the period without any reference to Rowley's House and Mansion. Both are named after William Rowley, admitted a burgess in 1594 and a business-partner of Richard Cherwell, a brewer of Hills Lane. Rowley's House is a timber-framed building of three storeys and attics. It was not a house, it was an industrial building, almost certainly that which was described as a 'vast great brewhouse' in 1635. The complex was once much larger, additional timber-framed ranges on its south side having been demolished in the 1930s to create Shrewsbury's first municipal car park. At the north end is Rowley's Mansion, built in 1616-18. This is one of the first brick houses built in the town, the use of brick having previously been confined to specific features, usually chimneys and fireplaces. Other outstanding examples of early brick architecture are the former Park Social Club in Horsefair, Abbey Foregate, and Scott's Mansion on Claremont Hill; both probably built c.1660-80. Another is the historic Loggerheads pub on Church Street, probably built in 1665. A generation later, by the 1690s, all polite building was in brick, though timber framing continued to be used by builders where it could not be seen from the street.

The Loggerheads building on the corner of Church Street and Dogpole. Probably built in 1665, this is one of the town's first-generation brick buildings. The pub interior is one of the finest in the region, untouched by modern breweries

The West End and the lost stream of Romaldesham

The part of the town centre that has fairly recently become known as the West End - centred on Barker Street, Hill's Lane and St Austin's Street - had a distinct identity in the Middle Ages. It was known as Romaldesham, supposedly named after the chapel dedicated to St Romald, an early Mercian infant prince, grandson of King Penda, which stood just to the north of where Rowley's House was built (however, the place name was a very ancient one and it is possible that the chapel took its name from the place, not the other way round). Archaeologically, this is the least well-known part of central Shrewsbury. Historical evidence fills in some of the gaps. It was a socially mixed area, with the halls of wealthy citizens scattered about amongst the tanning industry, one of the most noxious and polluting trades medieval towns had to offer. Tanners congregated in areas with a good supply of running water, and this one was no exception. Draining from the Gumbestolesmore, the pool and bog now under the Square (p.46), local tradition and antiquarian writers insist that there was a stream, known as the Gullet, that gave its name to Gullet Passage, and to an inn that used to stand there. This was said to have run along Mardol Head, down Claremont Street and Barker Street, St Austin's Street, and thence to the river. Although historical research has yet to find any evidence of a watercourse called 'The Gullet' in the Middle Ages, it is now becoming clear that there is, or was, a lost stream following roughly this course.

In 1932, Mr J A Morris, a local builder and Honorary Curator of the town museum, published an account of a stone culvert that discharged into the river just below the Welsh Bridge. It was, he said, large enough to walk up all the way to Mardol Head and was so wide at the river end that 'it may once have been the bed of a stream flowing into the river'. This culvert still exists, and was seen briefly by archaeologists in 1997 working ahead of the redevelopment of the site of the Augustinian Friary, in the area of the present Sixth-Form College and the present restaurants and night-clubs. An excavation trench placed alongside it found a section of the medieval town wall and a tower with what was probably a postern (pedestrian) gate. From it, a wall extended across the roof of the culvert and appeared to form one side of a small medieval bridge that had been built across the watercourse flowing beneath: when the culvert was built, the bridge was encapsulated in it. The topography of the area suggests that this watercourse formerly flowed in the old town ditch, into the river. Further upstream, local authority sewer plans show that the culvert, now of brick, runs up St Austin's Street and Barker Street two metres or more below the roadway.

Documentary evidence that has recently come to light suggests that there was indeed an ancient, open watercourse on this line. In 1527 the male householders of Romaldesham and Claremont Hill complained that 'because the canal is not made' (because the channel is not made up) 'it marryth all the street when any rain is'. A few years later the Romaldesham householders were demanding that the channel in the street should be paved so that the water could take its course, and that the 'spout's end' needed to be repaired in stone. There is not quite enough evidence yet to link this watercourse with the legendary 'Gullet' and thence to the pool under the Square, but a partial link was established in 1867 when a new sewer was being excavated down Claremont Street alongside the new Victorian market hall. About seven feet down, the workmen came across an open, timber-lined ditch filled with black mud and supported at intervals by a series of strong timber struts placed across it. This sounds exactly like open, timbered watercourses that have been excavated in a number of early

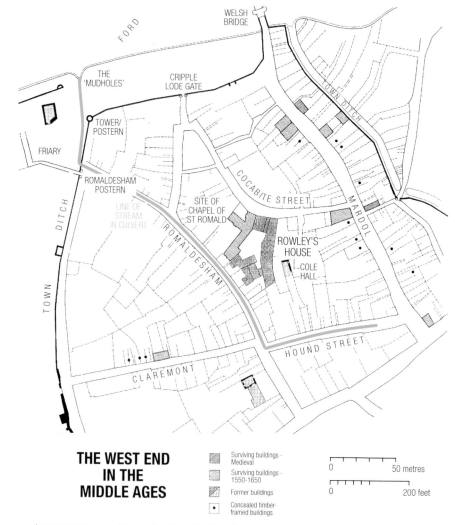

**THE WEST END
IN THE
MIDDLE AGES**

- Surviving buildings - Medieval
- Surviving buildings - 1550-1650
- Former buildings
- Concealed timber-framed buildings

0   50 metres

0   200 feet

A reconstruction map of the medieval Romaldesham district, the modern West End, centred on Barker Street and Mardol

medieval towns, Winchester for example, and suggests what the stream may have looked like prior to being culverted. This sequence of open natural watercourse, to canalised watercourse, to culverted (covered over) watercourse, to sewer, is a familiar one. It is, for example, exactly the process by which the minor rivers of London, such as the Fleet, disappeared. Such watercourses are also of immense archaeological importance. In the first place they were magnets for a variety of early activities and industrial processes - like tanning in Romaldesham/Barker Street. They also became receptacles for rubbish and waste, and in the permanently waterlogged, airless conditions that such channels provide, they can become a rich source of preserved, organic, archaeological finds, and evidence (from trapped seeds, pollen and wastes) for changes in the local environment and in people's diet. The Gullet - if that is what it is - remains an archaeological prize for the future, deep below the modernising West End.

Underground Shrewsbury

In the years either side of the First World War, a number of amateur archaeologists were to be found exploring cellars under the shops of the town centre. Their published reports were very brief, and tantalising. In 1913, for example, the Shrewsbury Chronicle reported on the activities of 'three men and a candle (and sometimes only a box of matches) the said three men being a committee of a learned Society appointed to investigate the remains of the town wall and mark them on a map, and thus secure a permanent record of them. The remains of our earliest wall are only to be found in the basements and cellars of modern houses, and on going into these lower regions they have discovered a wonderful series of cellars and vaults such as no other town can show.'

These men were the Town Walls Committee of the Caradoc & Severn Valley Field Club. They were looking for the remains of what was believed at the time to be an 'inner town wall' - lost medieval defences that pre-dated the construction of the well-known town wall of the 13th century. Their candle-lit explorations had been prompted by articles written in the 1880s by the Reverend Charles Henry Drinkwater, Vicar of St George's, Frankwell. Drinkwater was a keen historian who had noticed a massive sandstone wall running through the back yards of properties on the High Street (see picture, p.53). He traced it towards Pride Hill, running below Fish Street and Butcher Row, and thought he had found it again in the cellars of shops on the north-west side of Pride Hill. His theory (now disproved) sparked a wave of interest amongst the town's historical-archaeological enthusiasts, and for many years learned journals and local press columns carried accounts of 'ancient sandstone walls' in cellars throughout the town centre.

These stories (their maps are lost) were such an unknown quantity in the archaeology of the town that in 1996 a new programme of exploration took place, and more than 250 town-centre properties and their cellars were re-visited to see what they really contained. Just as reported, there are indeed many cellars in the town centre that contain ancient sandstone walls. In most cases, these turn out to be the remains of medieval undercrofts (basements for warehousing, storage, retailing or renting-out) to buildings that have long since been replaced at ground level - so it is not uncommon to descend a trap door in a Victorian shop into a 13th-century space beneath. Unusually, very few such undercrofts had the stone-vaulted roofs familiar in towns such as Chester; nearly all those in Shrewsbury had plain timber beamed ceilings. One stone barrel-vaulted undercroft survives beneath the Old Mansion, St Mary's Street (now part of the Prince Rupert Hotel), and there are records of three others elsewhere, all now demolished.

The earliest undercroft found so far is probably another cellar beneath the Old Mansion that appears to pre-date the much-disguised 14th-century timber hall on top. The sandstone walls seen under Pride Hill by the Reverend Drinkwater, and subsequently by the three men with a candle, were found again in the 1980s and identified as the remains of the undercroft of a very large medieval hall, of which there is no trace at street level, since sub-divided between four modern premises. It had been built c.1300 and had probably been part of a mansion belonging to a branch of the medieval Pride family, who gave their name to the street. Rarely visited, other than for meter-reading and boiler maintenance, the remains are trapped in the lower of two storeys of cellarage, cut into the hillside; when inspected the cellars still bore A.R.P. notices from their use as an air-raid shelter in the Second World War.

Not all stone walls in town-centre cellars are what they seem. Some, under the shops at the top of Wyle Cop, look medieval but are in fact of c.1800, built out of re-used masonry from demolished medieval buildings. Many cellars contain much more recent social history. Victorian cast-iron ranges are common, relics of a period when cellars were used as kitchens to cook for the families and staff working in the shops above. Others still have their gas lighting fixtures; one cellar was found still to have meter-reading cards from the Shrewsbury Corporation Electricity Works.

The remains of medieval cellarage, two levels down, deep below shops on Pride Hill

A medieval cellar or undercroft being recorded below a Georgian building on Butcher Row.
The brick arches support the 18th-century fireplaces on the floor above

The social history of cellars: a Victorian range and gas lighting, below a High Street shop

Tunnels

Conversations about Shrewsbury's past with local residents often lead on to stories of tunnels. Tunnels are said to go from one historic site to another (the abbey and the castle feature regularly) regardless of natural obstacles like the Severn, and have sometimes been explored 'by a friend', but never by the person speaking. Tunnels are embedded in the folklore that attaches to historic places; the question is, what truth, if any, lies behind such stories?

A number of common features of underground Shrewsbury give rise to tunnel stories. Cellarage has often been rented out separately from the premises above and doorways and passages inserted in cellar walls to give access from one property through to another. When memory of such arrangements is lost, such features may, once blocked off, give rise to speculative explanations. Cellars not infrequently extend out under the pavement and the road in front: either because the road has been widened since (as in parts of the High Street), or because there was no other way to accommodate Victorian coal cellars. A blocked entrance, or the occasional collapse caused by a passing lorry, again gives rise to speculative explanation. A fascinating case came to light in central Shrewsbury in the 1990s. In 1949 an elderly lady had written to the local press to report that she had been born in a town-centre house eighty-two years earlier (c.1867) and that there was a tradition that an underground passage led from it to the site of a nearby church. There was, she said, a door in the cellar that 'was always barred and nailed up' and this was said to be the entrance to the tunnel. When archaeologists were given access to the cellar they entered only to have their hopes dashed: it was a brick cellar with absolutely no unusual features and certainly no blocked door. However, some months later they were granted access to the cellar of an adjacent property. Leading from it, sideways and downwards,was a passage, roughly hacked through the masonry, into another low, brick-vaulted cellar at a much lower level. Measurements soon confirmed that they were in a cellar below the cellar previously inspected, and unknown to the occupants of the building above. The barred and nailed-up doorway reported in 1949 was almost certainly the access from the upper cellar to the lower cellar, whose existence appears to have been forgotten by the mid-19th century. The explanation for two-storey cellarage here, on a flat site with no hillside to dig into, may be related to the position of the property on a corner, with no back yard. The building of c.1700 over it may have been built for a wine merchant or other businessman who needed more cellarage than could easily be fitted into the plot, so the only way to go was down. Once memory of the lower cellar was lost, legend filled in the gap.

Real tunnels do, however, exist. One was found when building the Pride Hill Centre in 1986-7, leading from the town wall at the rear of the site to commercial cellarage on the Pride Hill frontage. It dated to the 1930s and was simply a passage built for the convenient movement of delivered goods from the yard behind straight into the stock-rooms. One genuine tunnel remains a mystery. In 1891 a builder working at the bottom of the town wall behind the Guildhall on Dogpole leant some planks against the wall, which collapsed to reveal the entrance to a tunnel. It was explored and mapped for 130 feet, up to the point where it was blocked, somewhere in the vicinity of the Guildhall. It was thoroughly examined in the 1890s and thought not to have been a drain, but no other credible explanation was forthcoming. The passage, about a metre high and built of brick with an arched roof, still exists but has been blocked off just within the entrance, which is still plainly visible from the bottom of the slope below.

Disused Victorian coal cellars projecting out under the pavement and the street from a building on Dogpole

A real Shrewsbury tunnel: the mysterious passage through the town wall below Dogpole, now blocked-off just within the entrance

The unsolved questions of early Shrewsbury

A great paradox lies at the heart of Shrewsbury's archaeology. The modern town is, for its size and given the vibrancy of its economy, extraordinarily well preserved. Along its ancient streets are literally hundreds of historic listed buildings dating from the 13th to the 19th century; some of them even retain medieval tiles on their roofs. Almost any town view would contain something that would be recognisable to a Salopian of the 16th century. But one of the consequences of this unusually fine state of preservation is that opportunities for development-led rescue excavations have been few and far between. The buildings of the late medieval, Tudor, and Georgian town protect and conceal the evidence of earlier centuries. The result is that there are still huge question marks over a number of important aspects of the town's origins and early development.

As the introductory section has indicated, the origins of Shrewsbury are particularly obscure. While it is thought that some of the earliest activity on the site of the town began at two churches, or rather monasteries, St Mary's and St Chad's, neither has been excavated since the 19th century. So whether they did indeed originate in the early 700s remains a matter for conjecture; what they looked like in their earliest centuries is totally unknown. And if, as suggested, there was a period when the river-loop was gradually transformed from a kind of monastic island into a town with a permanent population engaged in trade and in craft production - where and when did this happen? And for a town nationally famous for its historic buildings, we still have no complete excavated examples of any houses built before the first generation of buildings that still stand. Similarly, the defences of Saxon Shrewsbury have still not been located by excavation, though there are clues to their location. Even the medieval town walls have never been surveyed as a whole. At the castle, a monument of the greatest regional significance, archaeological investigation has only recently begun.

There are other areas of the town where virtually no excavation has ever taken place and whose development (in periods before documents become available) is a complete blank. The West End, the historic Romaldesham district, is one of these. Perhaps of even greater importance in this regard are the historic suburbs. Medieval Shrewsbury was not confined within the river loop. Abbey Foregate, Coleham, Frankwell, Coton Hill and Castle Foregate were all suburbs that grew up in the medieval period. The Foregate, now Abbey Foregate, certainly originated before the Norman Conquest, and on the analogy of other towns, Coton Hill may have been a pre-Conquest satellite settlement of cottage-dwelling day-labourers coming into town to seek employment. The suburbs were the 'growing edges' of the medieval and Tudor town, but how fast they grew and how, and what they were like, will never be known unless opportunities to excavate are taken before sites are redeveloped. Another question hangs over the origin of the bridges. The Severn crossings must always have been a crucial factor in the growth of the town, but when was the river first bridged? The mystery remains, and it is no comfort that in none of the other major historic towns of the Severn - Wroxeter, Worcester or Gloucester - is the chronology of bridge building known either.

And finally, the surviving medieval and Tudor buildings may be the jewel in the crown of Shrewsbury's historic environment, but they are also a source of information of immense importance about past townspeople and their lives. The routine recording of buildings when their structures are stripped down in the course of repair work, particularly if features are to be removed or covered over again for generations, is simple, fast - and essential. The essence of Shrewsbury's physical past is its multi-dimensionality. Historic buildings, their landscape setting of streets, plots, and terraces, the buried archaeology under them and the documents written about them and their owners, all form a continuum. All, together, in combination, illustrate how and why this town has remained in business for a thousand years.

An archaeological site evaluation in progress. A test trench being excavated by specialist contractors (Marches Archaeology Ltd) in 2001 on a development site in St Julian's Friars. Remains of the medieval town wall have been exposed in the end of the trench

Further Reading

Nigel Baker: Shrewsbury Abbey: a medieval monastery, Shropshire Books, 1998

Nigel Baker (ed.) Shrewsbury Abbey: studies in the archaeology and history of an urban abbey, Shropshire Archaeological and Historical Society, monograph series no.2, 2002

Nigel Baker: Shrewsbury: an archaeological assessment. English Heritage, forthcoming, 2005

Bill Champion: Everyday life in Tudor Shrewsbury, Shropshire Books, 1994

Dorothy Cromarty: Everyday life in Medieval Shrewsbury, Shropshire Books, 1991

Hobbs, J L, The street names of Shrewsbury, 1954 (reprinted)

Madge Moran: Vernacular Buildings of Shropshire, Logaston Press, 2003

Richard K Morriss and Ken Hoverd, The Buildings of Shrewsbury, 1993, Alan Sutton

Owen, H and Blakeway, J B, The History of Shrewsbury, 1825

Victoria History of Shropshire, vol.VI: Shrewsbury, eds. G C Baugh and D Cox, forthcoming

Internet and database resources

The primary source for archaeological sites and monuments in Shrewsbury is the Shrewsbury Urban Archaeological Database, a sub-set of the Shropshire County Sites & Monuments Record, maintained by the Natural & Historic Environment Team of Shropshire County Council, at the Shirehall, Abbey Foregate, Shrewsbury. The Shropshire SMR core data is also available online via the Archaeological Data Service. To access it, go to the Archaeological Data Service home page at http://ads.ahds.ac.uk then choose Arch Search Catalogue Holdings. To confine your search to the Shropshire SMR, choose Search then Search by Resource in the first instance.

The Shrewsbury Museums website at http://www.shrewsburymuseums.com provides information about displays, special exhibitions and events in Shrewsbury's museums: Shrewsbury Museum and Art Gallery (Rowley's House), Shrewsbury Castle and Shropshire Regimental Museum, Coleham Pumping Station. The 'Darwin Country' website at http://www.darwincountry.org is a rich resource of images and information about the social history, archaeology and natural history of Shrewsbury and Shropshire. It provides access to high quality images of pictures, archives, objects and specimens in the collections of Shrewsbury Museums Service and other partner museums, including Ironbridge Gorge Museum Trust. The site already contained some 10,000 pages and 9,000 images by April 2003. Information based on the Shrewsbury Urban Archaeological Database will be made available through Darwin Country from 2003, linking information from the SUAD with images of the sites from historic pictures (e.g. Shrewsbury Abbey in the 19th century) and images of objects associated with the sites (e.g. archaeological artefacts from excavations at the abbey). The new Shrewsbury Museums Service collections website 'ShrewD Online', to be made public in summer 2003 at http://www.shrewdonline.org, will provide additional information about the museum collections.

The author of this book can be contacted at nigel@lowerbrompton.freeserve.co.uk

Index